Tamil/ Transnationalism

A
"Convenient Concept"

Rajan Mahavalirajan

authorHOUSE®

AuthorHouse™
1663 Liberty Drive, Suite 200
Bloomington, IN 47403
www.authorhouse.com
Phone: 1-800-839-8640

First published by AuthorHouse 10/29/2009

ISBN: 978-1-4490-2006-4 (e)
ISBN: 978-1-4490-2004-0 (sc)
ISBN: 978-1-4490-2005-7 (hc)

Library of Congress Control Number: 2009911589

Printed in the United States of America
Bloomington, Indiana

This book is printed on acid-free paper.

This work is dedicated to my father, the late Mr. V. Ponnampalam.

General Secretary of
The Red Tamil Movement

"We are slaves of none."

Contents

Introduction

The defeat of the Liberation Tigers of Tamil Eelam in Sri Lanka has triggered many of us to wonder about the next phase of the Liberation movement. Tamil nationalism has gone through two different political stages in its native land and one beyond its borders. The first stage was the democratic process of the elected Tamil nationalist parties and the second was the recent growth and the downfall of Tamil militant nationalism. The last stage is currently unfolding international pressure initiated by the Tamil transnationalist.

In every stage of these developments, there were similarities in the nature of their operation. Basically, there were and are three groups that continue to play their respective roles: the middle class professionals with aspirations to achieve higher political statuses; the Tamil capitalists that support the operations of the nationalist movements; and lastly, the Tamil criminals, an organized group of underworld members carrying out all illegal aspects of the operation.

In the midst of all this, one will always find the most vulnerable members of Tamil Society, the common people of our country. They are victimized both by Tamil nationalism as well as Sinhala nationalism. Students certainly fall into this group; however, there are some who will evolve to any of the above three: the middle class professional, the organized criminal, or the capitalist.

The political drama that is played out by these actors continues to suppress the voice of Sri Lanka's working class irrespective of the ethnicities of its members. This drama is well-directed by the ethno-nationalists of the nation, while their interests continue to exist intact. An end to the ethnic conflict on the island is not desirable to the above three players. Ending it would soon end their existence; therefore, these three actors would like to continue the drama as a lifelong series.

Educating the vulnerable would possibly steer the direction of the events to reach moderation. This is my first endeavor; to educate the people in order to save them from victimizing themselves. I hope to see the working class of the country come out of racial division and see the issue beyond the context of race. It is my desire that they unite on the basis of economical class to end the conflict that continues to oppress the working class. The nation of Sri Lanka has been ruled with "organized lies"; it is about time to bring out the truth of the story that has been neglected and put aside in the form of "disorganized truth."

The Birth of Tamil Nationalism

Nationalism has played its role in shaping the political landscape of former colonial countries by uniting people beyond their ethnicity, religiosity and linguistic barriers. It has aimed at uniting them in fighting to win their independence from their colonial masters; however, it has not given any consideration to the political status of the various minorities within its national boundaries. Consequently, these liberated nations quickly plunged into a state of political chaos. In the midst of winning freedom, the colonized nations were blindly, as well as emotionally driven to establish an independent state constitution, which complicated the future politics of postcolonial nations. The South Asian region is a typical example to the above statement: the independence of India, instantly led to the independence of Pakistan and, subsequently, to the independence of Bangladesh.

However, the independence of Ceylon emerged with no defined political status for Northern Tamils, Eastern Tamils, Tamils living in the hill country and the Muslims of the island. Tamils living in the hill country were adversely affected as a result of the birth of the free and independent Ceylon. The united citizens of Ceylon, both the Sinhalese and the Tamils, jointly deprived the citizenship of the hill country Tamils that were considered to be of Indian origin.

At this point, it should be noted that the Northern Tamil politicians, who would emerge as Tamil nationalists longing for the support of the Tamils in Tamil Nadu, India, played a major role in bankrupting the Indian Tamils inhabiting the hill country of Ceylon. As a result, the birth of the new nation as Ceylon inherited political deformity. It failed to understand the ethnic, religious and linguistic diversity of the inhabitants of the island. It should also be noted that the Tamils, comprising 12.6% of the population, dominated the North and the East; the Sinhalese, comprising 74% of the population, dominated the South and West; the hill country Tamils, comprising 5.6% of the population, dwelt mainly in the central district; and finally, the Muslims at 7.1% of the population, were scattered in the North and the South. All of these groups had a distinct culture and language with the ability to administer them; moreover, they all had political aspirations for self-governance.

Lord Acton, one of the greatest thinkers of the nineteenth century, said: "A great democracy must either sacrifice self government to unity or preserve it by federalism."

"The co-existence of several nations under the same state is a test, as well as best security of its freedom. It is also one of the chief instruments of civilization.

The combination of different nations in one state is as necessary a condition of civilized life as the combination of men in society."

"Where political and national boundaries coincide, society ceases to advance, and nations relapse into a condition corresponding to that of men who would renounce intercourse with their fellow men.

A State which is incompetent to satisfy different races condemns itself; a State which labors to neutralize, to absorb, or to expel them, destroys its own vitality; a State which does not include them is destitute of the chief basis of self government. The theory of nationality, therefore, is a retrograde step in history."

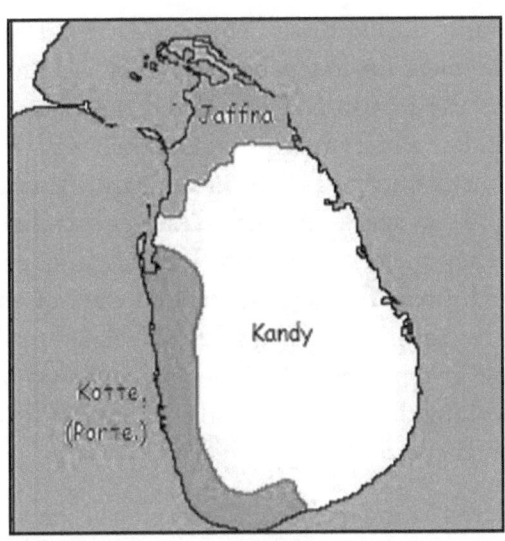

At the time of the arrival of the Portuguese,
there were three different rulers on the island.

In order to understand the political aspirations of Tamils, one has to look at the political powers that existed prior to the invasion of any foreign forces on the Island. The Island of Serendip, present-day Sri Lanka, had three different foreign rulers since the 16ᵗʰ century: the Portuguese who renamed it Ceilão, followed by the Dutch and lastly, the British who transliterated the Portuguese name to Ceylon. Also, at the time of the Portuguese's arrival, the Island had three different kingdoms: one in the North ruled by a Tamil king named Pararajasegaram, one in the South ruled by a Sinhala king, and one in the hill country ruled by a Nayakar (a caste from South India). The North and the South fell into the hands of foreigner invaders; however, the Nayakar continued to defeat all advancing foreign forces. The invasion by the British, after many attempts, toppled the last kingdom on the Island.

The aim of the British then was to unify the country in order to develop efficient commerce and political administration. As they unified the country, they introduced a common language for administration. The English traditions and customs became deeply rooted in the emerging new class of civil servants. This class included members of both the Tamil and Sinhalese ethnic groups. The race barrier disappeared in this class and they became connected by Western values. This class emerged as the class of civil servants during British rule and later evolved as nationalist politicians in the quest for independence. They were able to speak the same language as the British and negotiated their way out. While this elite class of Sinhalese and Tamils negotiated their way through this time, the majority of the country was kept in the dark. Almost 95 percent of the population did not speak English and never socialized beyond their ethnic groups. They merely listened to meaningless speeches delivered in English and admired the formally dressed class of elites. The issues of the commoners--Tamil or Sinhalese, never related to the issues of the elite class of these groups; thus, the independence won by the elite class of Ceylon had nothing to do with the real economic independence sought by common Tamils and Sinhalese.

Having achieved its independence without a vision for the social, political and economic condition of the country's future, the nation evolved to a communal form of politics that led to the development of Sinhala nationalism in the South, and Tamil nationalism in the North and East. This communal form of politics was an inevitable result of the nation's inability to cope with the economic needs of the country. The economic conditions that prevailed in the 1950s made many unemployed youth join the Marxist party with the hope of finding a remedy for their misery. The strong labor movement, along with the impoverished conditions of the common people of the Island and the unemployed frustrated youth, allowed for the Communists to flourish. Capitalism conveniently found the minority Tamils as their scapegoat; this was evident in the events surrounding the first communal riots of 1958. The formation of labor unions and their success in executing a general labor strike in the country had forced the servants of the capitalists to ignite the first communal riot, the result of which became a relentless force beyond the control of its creators. The consequences of this riot permanently disabled the workers' unity beyond ethnic barriers. This is clearly explained in the book *Emergency '58 – The Story of the Ceylon Race Riots* by Tarzie Vittachi: "There were politicians ready to encourage this brand of thinking and they lost no time in building this race awareness into a more erosive force. It began to be widely believed that the Tamils occupied an average of about 60 per cent of the places in the public service."

It is axiomatic from the election results that the country was slipping into communal-based political camps with separate parties for Tamils and Sinhalese. It is interesting to see that all the candidates of the Tamil nationalist parties, such as The Tamil Federal Party and the Tamil Congress, came from higher caste families with ample land ownership. However, the Karaiyar caste was the only lower caste that managed to take the next top-ranking position with the super grade Vellalar caste. Mr. C.X. Martin from Jaffna, Selathampu from Mullaitivu, and the late Mr. Thuriratnam from Point Pedro were all of the Karaiyar caste. This allocation of seats to the members of Karaiyar community was the only sensible choice in capturing the electorates that were traditionally held by the Marxist political parties and the parties that possessed some of the more charismatic leaders. The Tamil nationalist figured that the split of votes on the basis of caste was the only hope for their victory.

Allocation of seats to lower caste members was possible due to the greater number of Karaiyar voters in these electorates. This was also the last battlefield for Velupillai Pirabaharan (Prabhakaran). The last point of the battlefield was Kariyammullivacal. (The first part of the word Kariyam refers to the Karaiyar caste). One can also see that the higher caste candidates from Tamil nationalist parties were defeated in previous elections. The only hope was to create caste awareness among voters in order to win those electorates; thus, race manifestations and caste creations were both inventions of the capitalists to defeat the progressive forces among the Tamils.

Point Pedro was held by the most popular Communist leader, P. Kandiah. Kandiah was the only communist ever elected from the Tamil region of Sri Lanka. To capture a Tamil electorate that had identified itself with class awareness, the Tamil nationalist politicians embraced the idea of caste awareness. Caste awareness was able to create an emotional bond; a bond that was certainly stronger than the rational bond created by class awareness.

The growth of Tamil and Sinhala nationalist parties not only gave a new impetus for the growing separation among the citizens of Sri Lanka, but it also crushed the leftist movement. The emergence of ethno-nationalism has been reflected very well in the elections following independence. One can see the depletion of votes from the parties with no or less ethno-nationalism immediately resulting in an increase in the number of votes earned by those demonstrating ethno-nationalism. Similarly, one can also observe that as ethno-nationalism grew stronger, people became highly active in politics and took part in the elections. The 1977 election had the highest percentage of pooling. As citizens became highly engaged in politics, they began pressuring their politicians to act on the political promises they were making. The independent state for Tamils in Sri Lanka was based on such promises given by the Tamil nationalists. The Sinhala nationalist politicians also made promises of an electoral victory.

In addition to these political maneuverings by the nationalist politicians, the Buddhist Monks took up their fight to establish a Buddhist state. Unfortunately, the role played by the Buddhist monks in depriving the nation was regrettable and was subjected to condemnation. The absence of "divinity" in the actions of these monks undermined the slight possibility of a political settlement. As Swami Vivekananda stated, "Religion is the manifestation of the Divinity already in man.". The religion of these monks was not manifested from divinity.

Election results based on party standing		
Political Parties	1970 election	1977 election
UNP	17	140
SLFP	90	9
LSSP	19	
CP	6	
MEP		
TULF	13	18
TC	3	
EROS		
SLMC		
OTHERS	2	2

From the above chart, one can see that leftist parties, such as the Communists occupied 6 seats and the LSSP (Lanka Sama Samaja Party) captured 19 seats in the 1970 election. However, the rapid growth of ethno-nationalism among the Sinhalese and the Tamils totally rejected these Marxists ideologists. Despite this rejection, the Sri Lankan leftist parties failed to take a strong stand on the minority question. Of course, they passed new proposals in their committee meetings and debated on them. Ultimately, they always associated with Sinhala nationalist parties to secure more cabinet positions. They consistently attempted to assist their supporters with employment, settlements, promotions and transfers; however, it never occurred to them that they had to address the core problems of the country.

Their failure to identify and advocate a firm solution for the minority issue, coupled with their failure to force the Sinhala nationalists to consider a political solution, made them very unpopular among the Tamils. The support that was enjoyed by the Communist candidates in the Tamil region was a direct result of the personal influence and charm of the Tamil Communist political candidates. However, the personal qualities of those individuals failed to match the growing Tamil nationalism in the Tamil regions. The Southern area of the country had more unemployment and other economic issues that caused their youth to be more radical than the lecturing Communists. The youth in the South were keener to launch an arms struggle to overthrow the existing nationalist governments. As the Communists and other leftists remained partners with the ruling Sinhala nationalist government, the Communists became unpopular in Sinhalese areas. As a result of this condition, the Communists were totally annihilated in the democratic process. Ethno-nationalism aided by the capitalists flourished well through the following years. Along with this, capitalism grew rapidly and established an exclusive zone of foreign investments beyond the control of the local market conditions. The rebellion by Sinhalese youth was crushed by the nationalists while the leftists took the side of the Sinhala nationalists.

As ethno-nationalism reached the peak of the conflict, the country became highly political. This is evident from the voter turnout in the national elections.

Election year	Percent of Electorate Voting
1947	55.8
1952	70.7
1956	69.0
1960	77.6
1965	82.1
1970	85.2
1977	86.7
1982	70.8
1989	63.6
1994	76.2

Source: *Government And Politics in South Asia: Fourth Edition*

One can clearly see the evidence in the record-breaking electorate voting of 1977; the voter turnout was 86.7%. This election had the highest voter turnout in Sri Lankan history. The country dove headlong into ethno-nationalism as a means of electing their respective ethnic nationalist leaders and to reject the others.

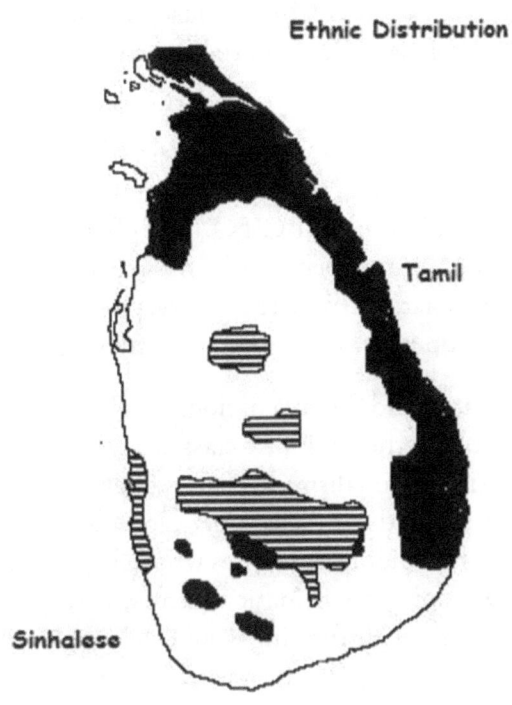

Ethnic Distribution

Tamil

Sinhalese

A clear ethnic divide exists in present-day Sri Lanka.

Thus, ethno-nationalism grew with the support of the Sinhala and the Tamil capitalist classes and they both, while opposing each other, shared a similar political goal. Their shared goal was to score the highest number of seats in the parliamentary elections. They both had to unify the people on the basis of race and caste. Efforts on the part of the Marxist parties to unify the people on the basis of class were outperformed by the strong emotional bond created by the race. The defeat of the Marxist parties certainly buried the aspirations of the underprivileged social class in Sri Lanka.

This idea of ethno-nationalism had evolved as a convenient concept for political opportunists as well as small businessmen who acted on their economic interests to capture a market that would exclusively serve their respective business interests. This was evident in the looting and burning of Tamil businesses in Sinhalese areas as well as the instances of Sinhalese bakery owners being chased out of Tamil areas and vice versa. This particular action was aimed at creating exclusive markets for the Sinhala businessmen in the Sinhala region and the same for Tamil businessmen in Tamil areas.

Historical events, such as the defeat of Elara (the last Tamil King of the central district of Sri Lanka who ruled central Sri Lanka with Anurathapuram as his capital from 205BC TO 161 BC) in a battle against the Singhalese king, Dutahimunu, became the masterpiece to stimulate any dying Tamil or Sinhala nationalism. This masterpiece would conveniently appear in Sri Lankan politics as and when needed.

The growth of Tamil and Sinhala nationalism inherited three groups of players; the first being the capitalist class from both ethnicities that funded their respective nationalism; the second being the criminals that carried out any and all kinds of illegal operations; and the third group, which was, of course, the middle class elites who held political aspirations. The function of the capitalists in nationalism was to provide funding with the expectation that their funding would yield higher returns in the future as their party secured political status. The criminals were able to carry out the necessary illegal activities to secure places for their respective nationalist leaders. In return, they would expect a concession or exclusion from some of their major criminal charges. The criminals would also seek a future place in a legitimate business or even in politics. For example, in the area of Tamil nationalist politics, Kuttimani, who was a smuggler, became a celebrated national hero. The former Sri Lankan president, Pramadasa, in the Sinhala nationalist political arena was axiomatic to criminal politics.

Tamil as well as Sinhala nationalist politicians, who were primarily middle class elites and lawyers by profession, were skilled to manipulate the masses while blending the necessary amount of capitalists and criminals into the mix in order to achieve their goal. Creating rumors and proliferating them for the purpose of achieving their political goals was another inborn talent of these nationalist politicians as is evidenced by the rumors they propagated, such as one recorded in *Emergency '58*: "The female teacher from Panadura, the story went, who was teaching in a school in the Batticaloa District, had been set upon by a gang of Tamil thugs. They had cut off her breasts and killed her. Her body was being brought home to Panadura for cremation." However, the inspector of the school investigated and reported that there was no female teacher from Panadura on the staff of any school in the Batticola District.

These kinds of reports are not uncommon in modern Sri Lanka as we can clearly see with the story of five Tamil doctors serving on the battlefield of Vanni who issued many reports claiming that great numbers of Tamil civilian causalities were caused by the Sri Lankan armed forces. However, the same doctors had recently released a report saying that they were under constant pressure from the Liberation Tigers of Tamil Eelam (LTTE) to issue reports blaming the Sri Lankan government. As we all know, these doctors are currently in Sri Lankan government custody and this new report could be the result of the Sri Lankan government's coercion. False political propaganda continues to dominate the Sri Lankan press and the majority of the population fall victim to it.

It has been a one-of-a-kind experience that the Tamils and the Sinhalese of Sri Lanka have endured since the end of colonial rule. Tamil nationalism, instead of uniting the Tamil-speaking people of Sri Lanka, has created a major division among the Tamils in Sri Lanka, ultimately defeating the very purpose for which it was said to be created. The Tamil language had not only played the role of medium for Tamil nationalism but also became the substance on which nationalists thrived in misleading the nation. The rise of nationalism in many colonized countries used race, religion and historical facts to unite the members of their nations. The Sri Lankan Tamils used their linguistic differences to distinguish themselves from the majority Singhalese without giving due consideration to the existing inequality among "Tamils." There were Tamils who were Muslims, Eastern Tamils, Tamils who were still subjected to the same substandard living conditions as plantation workers, and Tamils who were considered to be of a low caste and underwent an institutionalized and unjustified exploitation.

The "superior" class of Tamils had to come up with an idea that would drug and blind the exploited class of Tamils from seeing the real differences between them; the Tamil language became that substance – the opium for Tamil nationalism. However, the true colors of the exploiting class could not fail to appear now and then. One example of this was the anti-Muslim campaign, which entirely deprived Tamil Muslims of their belongings and drove them out of the Tamil region to the South of the country where the Muslims continue to this day to live as refugees. This was carried out with a notice from the Liberation Tigers of Tamil Eelam (LTTE), a Tamil nationalist militant group, for them to vacate their homes within forty-eight hours. The Muslims are still confined to camps in a distant region; hence, Tamil repatriates who are urging the international community to help their own people should also consider pleading for the displaced Muslims.

Tamil nationalism has created a false consensus among different groups of Tamil-speaking people to hide the existing inequality and to carry out the political agenda of the exploiting class. Such inequality will certainly evolve as a mighty force and divide "Tamil Eelam" into several smaller nations, unless the union of these smaller nations was to transform into a lasting consensus.

At this juncture, it is appropriate to view the thoughts of one of the greatest Canadian political thinkers, Pierre Elliott Trudeau, who once said, "the principle of national self-determination, which had justified their birth could just as easily justify their death. Nationhood being little more than a state of mind, and every sociologically distinct group within the nation having a contingent right of secession, the will of the people was in constant danger of dividing up – unless it were transformed into a lasting consensus."

Although, presently, many Tamils from the North would consider Karuna to be a traitor for the Tamil cause, one would certainly agree with the argument that the Northern Tamil politicians have always ruled over the political aspirations of the Eastern Tamils. Uniting the North and the East as one political unit would need to be addressed according to the viewpoint of Eastern Tamils. The political will of the Eastern Tamils should be respected and honored. The ruling mentality of the Northern Tamils and their superiority complex over Eastern Tamils as well as the hill country Tamils, will only lead to future regional political conflicts. The nation is not ready for another racial or regional conflict; hence, all regional issues should be addressed immediately.

Tamil Congress, the Tamil federal party and many other Tamil militant groups should have made attempts to strengthen Tamil nationalism as and when they were faced with Sinhala nationalism from the South.

The growth of Tamil nationalism included every segment of Tamils, and Tamil nationalism became a safe haven for traditional smugglers, arms dealers, and drug dealers; and more recently, international human traffickers Repatriated Tamil business owners, criminals and political opportunists, who were blessed as national heroes, came to represent Eelam Tamils from the various Tamil regions of Sri Lanka.

The emergence of local militancy in Tamil nationalism was first recognized with the murder of Alfred T. Durayappah, Mayor of Jaffna. In order to understand the origin of Tamil militancy, one has to understand the circumstances that existed to provide fertile ground for it to sprout. The following charts reveal the strength of Durayappah in the elections starting from 1960.

Jaffna Election March 19th 1960

A.T. Durayappah	Sun	6,201	24,299
G.G. Ponnambalam	Bicycle	5,312	
S. Kathiravelupillai	House	5,101	
Arulambalam Visuvanathan	Key	767	

Alfred T. Durayappah was a charismatic leader known for his friendly nature, elected for his personality and not for his political views. He stood as a challenge for the Tamil nationalists.

Jaffna Election March 22nd 1965

G.G. Ponnambalam	Bicycle	9,350	28,473
C.X. Martyn	House	6,800	
Alfred T. Duryappah	Pair of Scales	5,918	

Jaffna Election May 27th 1970

C.X. Martyn	House	8,848	31,214
A.T. Durayappah	Umbrella	8,792	
G.G. Ponnambalam	Bicycle	7,222	

The 1965 elections clearly show that the deployment of Karaiyar caste's C.X Martin to divide voters from Durayappah resulted in the victory of a Tamil nationalist candidate. As caste awareness overtook the natural charm of Durayappah, the Karaiyar caste-based candidate took the top of the podium. Although the progressive voice of one such as Durayappah was defeated in the parliamentary elections, his existence gave strong resistance to the growing Tamil nationalist politicians. For them, murdering him had become the only option to remove this electoral defeat.

The Tamil nationalists joined forces with the criminal element to murder Durayappah. As he approached the entrance of a Hindu temple to worship, his life was taken in cold blood. The fact that this great man's death occurred on the grounds of a Hindu temple, despite the fact that he was a Christian, demonstrates his wider acceptance of the diversity that existed beyond his tradition. The contention of the Tamil nationalists was that the mayor, on a previous occasion, had acted against the interests of the Tamil nation by ordering law enforcement officials to control a crowd that had been acting irresponsibly. As the officers tried to gain control over the crowd, shots were fired into the air striking overhead electrical wires. The wires fell among the crowd and injured some of the attendees. As a result of this incident, Durayappah was labeled a traitor. According to S. Ponniah, in his publication *The Truth vs. This is the Truth*, "The shooting of Durayappah was, probably, for two reasons: 1. that he was largely responsible for the police violence at the Tamil Conference and nine Deaths. 2. That he was, from the point of the militant youths, not true to the Tamil cause".

The second reason Ponniah gives was the most prominent one for his murder. The alienating and demonizing of a politician was the first strategy the Tamil nationalist politicians would employ before annihilating their political opponents for good. In the case of Alfred T. Durayappah, they accomplished this, firstly, by failing to issue him an invitation to the Tamil conference and secondly, by blaming him for the violence that occurred there. The frustrated Tamil nationalist politicians were searching for something to come along as a viable excuse to murder him, and the accidental deaths of those nine Tamils became the best event to stimulate the anti-Alfred feeling and demonize his personality; it also became their excuse to assassinate him.

It should be noted that the mayor was elected by Jaffna Tamils and continued to be a celebrated figure among the Tamils as well as in the Sri Lankan politics. His contribution to the city was remarkable and continued to gain mass support from the people. Tamil nationalism invented and disseminated caste awareness among the Jaffna Tamils to defeat Durayappah. Despite these political manifestations of caste, he continued to thrive as a leading politician in Jaffna. The Tamil national parties not only stayed silent on the murder of Durayappah, but also came forward to defend the accused in the murder trial. One of the accused was V. Pirabakaran, the leader of Liberation Tigers of Tamil Eelam.

Durayappah was not the only politician who emerged as a political rival for the Tamil nationalists. The former Member of Parliament from Vaddukoddai, the late Dr. Thiagarajah, was gunned downed for his association with Sri Lankan national parties, and the late Mr. Venothan was assassinated in Colombo. Recently, the Minister of Social Services, the Honorable Douglas Devanantha, was almost killed many times by suicide bombers. One has to see that these Tamil politicians had different approaches to the ethnic problem. Dr. Thiagarajah should be remembered for his sincere commitment to the well-being of his native land, his honesty and his brave approach toward his political opponents. It should also be noted that he was one of the drafters of the Tamil Eelam map.

The non-Tamil nationalist politicians focused on the development of their region and employment opportunities for their youth; they associated and negotiated with their Sinhala counterparts for these developments. Similarly, the LTTE had several talks with the Sinhala governments for issues that had nothing to do with the political rights of Tamils. If one would label this act as a betrayal to the Tamil cause, one is certainly obligated to explain the actions of the LTTE. The LTTE spoke of disarming the Karuna group--the rival faction of the LTTE in the Eastern part of the Tamil region. They negotiated with the government to obtain medical treatment for "Thaya Master", one of their leaders. Lastly, they even discussed terms for surrendering, and the list continues to grow. Do they have anything to do with the Tamil cause? The LTTE have engaged in talks many more times than parliamentary Tamil politicians; yet, the

LTTE called the non-LTTE Tamil politicians "traitors" and enemies of the Tamil cause.

Perhaps it is here that I should introduce my father, the late Mr. V. Ponnampalam, secretary of the Northern Communist Party and the candidate for the United Front--a coalitions of the Communist Party, the Sri Lanka Freedom Party and the Lanka Sama Samaja Party. V. Ponnampalam stood against the Tamil nationalist parties in many elections right up until the 1975 by-election. The 1977 election was the one that brought the Tamil parties together and further strengthened Tamil nationalism. The 1975 by-election was the turning point of my father's political life. This was the election that brought the Tamil nationalists into one united camp, and this was the election that made Ponnampalam question his dedication to the Communist Party of Sri Lanka.

As a child, I still remember the night my father was engaged in a meeting with delegates from the United Front at the Kankasenthuri Guest House. The representative from the Sri Lanka Freedom Party and one of the Tamil ministers, the late Mr. Kumarasuriyer, expressed that the Sri Lanka Freedom Party did not approve regional autonomy for Tamils or the "Five Point Solution" put forward by the Communist Party. Despite the fact that the Communist party of Sri Lanka had passed regional autonomy as the solution for the Tamil political problem and printed thousands of notices and wallpaper banners, all of which were burnt in front of my eyes in the front yard of our house. I can well imagine that that would have been a difficult night for my father. He was supposed to have filed his nomination as the United Front candidate the following morning. Standing in the election without having to put forward any political solution was not an easy task. However, pressure from the Communist Party, the promise the Communist Party had made to resolve the problem in three months time, as well as his long standing commitment to them made him file the nomination.

This is an example that clearly shows that the Communist party of Sri Lanka was sacrificing its own agenda just for the purpose of holding a few cabinet positions in parliament. It was in this election that my father lost his faith in the party, particularly in the leadership. The failure of the Communists to stand firm on the issue of Tamils was a huge political mistake. The Communist party was afraid of losing their support among the majority Sinhalese. Despite their fear, the Communists lost their traditional grip on labor unions as the labor issue became a secondary problem to ethno-nationalism, which took top place in the country's politics. V. Ponnampalam was labeled as a Tamil traitor for contesting the leader of the Tamil United Liberation Front. For his protection, the government issued him a revolver and a personal bodyguard. His bodyguard's name was Balasuriya, a sub-inspector who worked at the Chunnakam police station.

This was the period when Tamil youth became active in violent politics; not something that evolved naturally among the Tamils. Rather, it was instigated by the Sinhala nationalists and the criminal elements in Sinhala nationalist politics. Every race riot in the South and the number of refugees landing on the doorsteps of the Northern Tamils became the fertilizer for growing Tamil militant nationalism. In the midst of the growing tension, my father began questioning the Communist Party and openly criticized its failed role to bring a solution to the Tamil political problem as promised. Being the secretary of the Northern region of the Communist Party, he warned that the Communist Party would function as an independent body: this was released to the press. The Sinhala-dominated leadership of the Communist party became furious over this statement and convinced one senior member in the Northern region to reject this report. The Communist party fired Mr. Ponnampalam: I would imagine that this moment in his life was not something he ever anticipated.

Mr. Ponnampalam did not join the Communist party in Sri Lanka but started his membership in Madras, India where he completed his undergraduate studies and graduate studies at Madras Christian College. He got admitted to Madras Christian College on the recommendation of S.J.V. Chelvanayagam who was the leader of Tamil Federal Party and subsequently became the leader of the Tamil United Liberation Front. The late Mr. Chelvanayagam was a barrister in the Queens Council and a member of the Sri Lankan parliament for the Kankasenthuri electorate. Mr. Ponnampalam worked for Chelvanayagam during his election. The rationale was that the federal party was regarded as a progressive one in comparison to the Tamil Congress.

Upon returning from Madras, a number of changes were evident in Mr. Ponnampalam. He had originally been a Tamil federalist; however, he returned as a Communist and joined the Communist Party in Ceylon. He was a supporter of S.J.V. Chelvanayagam but returned as Chelvanayagam's opponent. He even returned to Ceylon as a meat eater though he had been a dedicated vegetarian prior to his journey to Madras. It was Madras that reformed and revived him as a new person. The impoverished conditions that existed in India and his volunteer work providing haircuts for the neglected as well as marginalized people of Madras caused him to embrace a Marxist ideology. During his exile in Madras in the early 1980's, he worked for an organization called "Roof for the Roofless". This organization was set up by his Guru, the late Professor Chandran Davanesan.

Mr. Ponnampalam became the candidate for the Communist Party and the political opponent of Chelvanayagam. Despite their political rivalry, Ponnampalam held Chelvanayagam in high regard. Moreover, there was an interesting twist to his political life following the defeat in the by-election of 1975: he started a political party called Senthamilar Iyakkam. The word "Senthamilar" means "pure Tamil" and the first part of the word "Sen" implies the color red; thus, the political movement came to be known in English as the Red Tamil Movement. Unfortunately, their lack of resources could not sustain the party long enough to create any positive impact. As a result, Ponnampalam became frustrated and left the political life that he had cherished for more than 30 years. After teaching for a few years in Lusaka, Zambia, he returned to Sri Lanka in early the 80's and joined the Tamil nationalist camp for Tamils' rights. This move was not welcomed by his supporters, including myself. Being associated with the Red Flag from childhood, it became difficult for me to change colors.

The following speech was delivered in the Sri Lankan Parliament by the opposition leader, the late Mr. A. Amirthalingam: "This was the statement that Mr. Chelvanayakam made on the Floor of the House on 3rd October 1972 when he resigned his Seat in order to give an opportunity for the then Government to test its claim that the Tamil people accepted the Constitution. Of course, the election was postponed for two years or more, and ultimately when the election was held in 1975 the voters of the Kankesanthurai Electorate, whom I have the privilege of representing today, gave an unequivocal verdict. And what was the verdict? By over 75 percent of the votes they returned Mr. Chelvanayakam, thereby not only indicating that they rejected the Constitution but also stressing what Mr. Chelvanayakam immediately after his victory in the election said, namely, 'I consider the verdict at the election as a mandate that the Tamil Eelam nation should exercise the sovereignty already vested in the Tamil people and become free.' In fact, the verdict is almost 100 percent today because the only candidate whom the then Government could persuade to contest Mr.Chelvanayakam on that issue, Mr. V. Ponnambalam of the Communist Party, has not given it up and has joined 'hands with the TULF in the struggle for the liberation of the Tamil people."

Following this, the Honourable Minister, the late Mr. Lalith Athulathmudali queried, "Has he left the Communist Party?

A.Amirthalingam: Yes, he has left the Communist Party. Acting on this mandate that the Tamil people gave, the Members of the TULF who were then in Parliament gave notice of a Private members' Motion. By a strange coincidence that appeared on the Order Paper of this House on the 4th of February, 1976."

There was a second close friend my father cherished, the late Mr. Tharmalingam, who was the Member of Parliament for the Tamil United Liberation Front from Uduvil. It was customary for him to come for tea at our house before his election nomination. His car would be parked in front of our house with the TULF flag. The level of respect and friendship that existed among them, beyond their political differences, was remarkable. This kind of political life was rare for modern Sri Lankan politicians.

Tharmalingam was gunned down, along with Mr. Alalasundaram, by a Tamil militant group. There was a dispute over who was responsible. Some believe, it was the work of the LTTE and others suspect the TELO (Tamil Eelam Liberation Organization).

Uduvil Election March 19th 1960

Visuvanathar Tharmalingam	House	9,033	27,278
P. Nagalingam	Key	3,811	
V. Ponnampalam	Star	3,541	
J.D. Asservatham	Book	1,552	
S. Handy Perimbanayagam	Pair of Spectacles	1,241	
N. Sivanesan	Sun	1,008	
V. Veerasingham	Cockerel	312	

This was the election in which my father, the late Mr. V. Ponnampalam, ran against his dear friend in the Uduvil electorate and lost. Mr. Ponnampalam always stood as the Communist Candidate. Although, the late Mr. Tharmalingam was elected as a Member of Parliament with the Federal Party and, subsequently, with the Tamil United Liberation Front, he was always regarded as a Marxist in the Tamil Federal Party. He was well regarded for his humbleness and honesty.

Kankesanthurai Election May 27th 1970

S.J.V. Chelvanayakam	House	13,520	37,804
V. Ponnampalam	Star	8,164	
C. Suntharalingam	Cockerel	5,788	
T. Thirunavakkarasu	Bicycle	3,051	

The 1970 election was considered to be a close call for defeating the Federal Party in Kankasenthuri, despite the final results. Following this election, there were a number of threats that were made on my father's life. Our house was bombed while my father was addressing a public meeting in Chunnakam in the Jaffna District along with the Prime Minister Mrs. Sirimavo Ratwatte Dias Bandaranaike. A dynamite bomb packed in the ventilation hole of the front office room of this bungalow house went off as I, along with my grandmother, were about to have dinner. The structure of the house was damaged; however, it failed to detonate the house as the placement of the bomb lacked technical accuracy. The bomb that was placed in a ventilation hole in the front room office of our house was not properly sealed to ensure maximum damage to the structure. Flying debris from the blast hit a large framed picture of Joseph Stalin but only the glass was broken; however, Joseph Stalin stood in front of my eyes with his majestic look. In the midst of that smoke covered darkness, I was impressed to see him in the lantern light. I regarded him as a supernatural figure that could save us.

The failure of the Tamil nationalist politicians to condemn the murder of Mr. Durayappah, and appearing as legal counsel for the accused with political interests inaugurated the violent political exercise that our nation continues to experience. One would be able to understand this clearly by looking at the electoral position of Tamil nationalists and their opposing political parties. It could also be seen as a drastic landslide victory for the Tamil nationalists as they proclaimed an independent Tamil state. Sinhala nationalists also had an equally appealing Sinhala race awareness campaign to crush Tamil nationalism. Sinhala and Tamil nationalists confronted each other in action, but ultimately complimented each other with their political goals. The growth of these two extreme nationalists curtailed and eliminated the growth of any prudent political parties among the Sinhalese as well as the Tamils. Tamil leftists as well as Sinhala leftists became unpopular for their failed role in communal politics. Furthermore, they were totally isolated as they failed to advocate a strong policy for the country's ongoing and ever-expanding Tamil and Sinhala nationalism. Sinhala nationalism was given the royal treatment as it enjoyed the backing of the state. Tamil nationalism had to grow with the support of Tamil nationalist politicians, resources in the Tamil criminal world and some obscure politicians from the neighboring Tamil Nadu, India.

While Tamil Nadu, India started keeping the militant Tamil baby in its incubator, the capital of the colonial master, London, England, became the international information center for militant Tamil nationalism. As several militant Tamils were exposed to the rest of the world, they were influenced by various ideologies and deviated from traditional Tamil nationalistic thinking. These ideologies along with personal disputes among members caused divisions in the Tamil militant group. The breakaway factions, evolving as militant Tamil organizations, covered comprehensive political and social agendas. A typical example for this would be the involvement of the PLOTE (People's Liberation Organization of Tamil Eelam) in the resettlement work of hill country Tamils in the North. The PLOTE was engaged in this social work under the guise of "Gandhiyam". The development of Tamil nationalistic militancy and revolutionized militancy with a comprehensive agenda became rivals as they represented two opposite factions. Nationalist militants associated with and represented wealthy upper middle class Tamils and with business owners. On the contrary, the second militant group associated with and represented the lower class and the lower caste Tamils. The nationalistic camp outperformed the revolutionized camp, and the end result made the Tamil nationalistic camp the dominant force. The members of the defeated group of Tamil militants defected to the government and agreed to work through their differences within the parliamentary system; some were stationed in India and others left for the Western world. The evolution of Tamil militancy continued even within traditional nationalistic militancy. Several other factions emerged; many were killed or expelled for future execution and few were lucky enough to escape.

Tamil nationalist militants assassinated the traditional Tamil national political party leader, A. Amirthalingam, who once enjoyed the status of an oppositional party leader in Sri Lanka. Although it is undeniable that the assassinated leader was one of the pillars of militant Tamil nationalism, the assassination not only terminated the status of the first Tamil leader of the opposition, but also ended the only legitimate voice of the Tamil nation. The absence of such an elected leader permanently created a political vacuum in legitimate leadership. The assassination of the opposition leader never ended the campaign on rooting out so-called "traitors." The campaign went on to find many within nationalistic militants. Basically, the act of rooting out any political opponents deemed "traitors" included anyone who ever questioned the leadership, anyone who ever accepted the head role of India in the conflict, or anyone who ever disputed over personal issues. As Tamil nationalism grew, it impacted the social, economic and political conditions of Sri Lanka as well as spilling over to other nations. In particular, neighboring India and the Western states with liberal immigration policies became the hot spot for Tamil nationalism.

Vaddukoddai Election March 22<u>nd</u> 1965

A. Amirthalingam	House	15,498	36,935
K. Subramaniam	Bicycle	4,359	
Arunasalam Thampipillay	Umbrella	4,082	
I.R. Ariaratnam	Star	1,561	

Vaddukoddai Election May 27<u>th</u> 1970

A. Thiagarajah	Bicycle	14,359	35,812
A. Amirthalingam	House	13,634	

As Tamil nationalism grew with the aid of militancy, Dr. A. Thiagarajah became the next hinderance. Thiagarajah was a teacher by profession and a dedicated, honest worker. He was born in Karrinagar, my mother's home town, a village in the Vaddukoddai electorate; this village is an island. The land is not fertile for traditional farming; thus, almost all of its inhabitants are small business owners in the Sinhala-dominated regions of Sri Lanka. Most of them are well-to-do financially speaking; however, they have high political aspirations for their Member of Parliament. Dr. Thiagarajah, a highly educated, honest and service-minded person who had entered the spotlight.

The victory of Thiagarajah was a victory for Karrinagar. He was able to change the economic landscape of his people by securing many government employment opportunities. During his time in office, there were a number of young educated members from Karrinagar that got their appointments in non-traditional forms of employment. They became teachers and telecommunication technicians, and worked in many other government service industries. This group of young, educated, politically active people became highly devoted to the late Dr. A. Thiagarajah. The support of these newly-emerged civil servants became the bastion for Thiagarajah. This electorate was an important one for the Federal Party as it housed Amirthalingam. Once again the Tamil nationalists faced a challenge that could not be won through the democratic process.

Consequently, the Tamil militants came to their aid by executing Thiagarajah.

One can clearly see that Tamil nationalism did not flourish on its own. It was able to grow with the support of Sinhala nationalists and their failed role in resolving the Tamil political issue: this chapter of Tamil democratic nationalism peaked under the leadership of Amirthalingam. He was considered to be an honest and brave political leader and was dubbed "the General" of the Tamil Nationalist Party. Under his remarkable leadership, he unified most of the remaining opposing Tamil politicians, captured the entire Northern region for the Tamils and positively impacted the East. He became the first Tamil leader of the opposition in the Sri Lankan Parliament. He was able to win the 1977 election with a landslide victory and unified the North and East under one nationalist camp. However, his achievements were unacceptable to the LTTE and he was assassinated in his Colombo residence along with other party leaders. The LTTE condemned the act of negotiating with the Sri Lankan government; however, they were engaged in many negotiations with the government until they were isolated within a few kilometer radius of Vanni. They cried out for negotiations even as they stood to face their last bullet.

The period under Chelvanayagam's leadership was a time of non-violent protests, and it was the beginning of Tamil nationalism along with conflicting views and equal resistance from many other Tamil politicians. The period under the leadership of Amirthalingam was a mixture of non-violence and violence. He was able to unify most of the Tamil politicians while some of his political opponents were being killed. He managed to keep the respect of the militants during the early part of his leadership; however, he himself became a victim of the militants.

Following his murder, Tamil nationalists resorted to a non-violent path of politics. Non-violence peaked under the leadership of Prabaharan and even extended its activities beyond the political borders of Sri Lanka. How Tamil nationalism grew along with Sinhala nationalism can only be explained by analyzing the nature and context of government policies and their amendments following the pressure of the nationalists.

One should first examine the case of the Sri Lankan Language Policy in which the elected SLFP (Sri Lankan Liberation Front Party) enacted the "Sinhala Only Act" in 1956. Although the former Prime Minister, S.R.D. Bandaranaike, took the entire blame for it, one should be aware that it evolved as a result of pressure from the opposing Sinhala nationalist parties. One could give some credit to the Marxists for opposing the act but certainly not forgive their continued association with Sinhala nationalists such as the SLFP.

The country had a definite need for resolving the language policy imposed by the British rulers. During the years 1830 to 1833, the English language became the official language, which meant that the nation's civil administration, court procedures, correspondence and communications were all done in English. This led to the development of an English-speaking middle class brokering civil matters between the majority of common people of the country and the government. The leader of the SLFP had made a promise that he would bring about changes to this issue. The policy he advocated was termed, "Suyabhasawa", which means "native language".

Problems arose as the debate escalated on the choice of language: which language should be considered for the official language status? Dispute resulted in accord and it was signed by both Prime Minister Bandaranaike and Chelvanayagam. The leader of the United National Party, the late Mr. Jayewardene, who later staged the famous Kandian March and destroyed the federal state form of government for Tamils, insisted that Sinhalese should be the only official language. Due to his fear of losing the national election, Bandaranaike abrogated the agreement. This was the first overt display of unwillingness of the Sinhala nationalists to resolve the Tamil ethnic problem.

Thus, the failure of the Sri Lankan government to act to resolve the Tamil issue was a direct cause of competing Sinhala nationalist parties. As the British united the Island's political administration into one centralized body, it required the administration to have a common language. The most common language for Tamils and Sinhalese happened to be neither Tamil nor Sinhalese: English had become the most common language for both, and convenient for their colonial master, the British. As with most colonized nations, the common language is usually a foreign language for the majority of the population.

The Native Language Policy was not a bad idea since, according to the 1946 Ceylon census, the country only had a 0.2% English-speaking population, a 2.9% English and Sinhalese-speaking population, and a 1% English and Tamil-speaking population. The developments from the very fine idea of native language only fueled the burning race-based politics. Ultimately, the native language policy did not help the common people to understand each other; it only served to provoke them to stage communal violence in the name of native language rights.

The disengagement of Tamils in civil functions became an unavoidable consequence. The "Sinhala Only Act" was the work of Sinhala nationalists aiming to capture the Sinhala voters: "The law had its intended effect. In 1955 the civil service had been largely Tamil; by 1970 it was almost entirely Sinhalese, with thousands of Tamil civil servants forced to resign due to lack of fluency in Sinhala. For much of the 1960s government forms and services were virtually unavailable to Tamils, but this situation improved with later relaxations of the law".

The second government policy that played a role in escalating the ethnic conflict was the "Standardization Policy". The real purpose of this educational policy was to allow more access to the limited spaces in post-secondary institutions to those who came from the underdeveloped areas of the country. Unlike the Western world, admission to Sri Lankan post-secondary institutions is highly competitive and due to the greater advantages in the urban centers, students from the larger cities continued to occupy the seats while students in rural and village schools continued to score less and were unable to pursue higher education. Consequently, the government had to take proactive measures to create an equal playing field.

The "Standardization Policy" was one such policy that aimed at bringing this change. In this context, the Northern district did not qualify for this privileged selection process; however, the Eastern district, which houses the majority of the Tamil population, was able to enjoy this privilege. This positively affected the majority of Sinhalese, as they mostly dwelled in the less developed areas, though it negatively affected the Jaffna Tamils in the Northern district. "30% of university places were allocated on the basis of island-wide merit; half the places were allocated on the basis of comparative scores within districts and an additional 15% reserved for students from under privileged districts. In 1969, the <u>Northern Province</u>, which was largely populated by Tamils and compromised 7% of the population of the country, provided 27.5 percent of the entrants to science based courses in Sri Lankan universities. By 1974, this was reduced to 7%. However, the hardest hit population groups were [sic] the urban Sinhalese in the <u>Western Province</u>, which contained 26% of the islands [sic] population. In 1969, the Western Province provided 67.5 percent of admissions to science based courses. This reduced to 27% in 1974, after the law came into effect."

Anyone viewing the above numbers would clearly understand that the policy was not aimed at preventing Tamils from entering higher studies; but, the policy put the most influential Tamils in a disadvantaged position. In particular, the Jaffna Tamils became the second largest group to be affected by this policy next to the urban Sinhalese in the Western province. Thus, the policy was not an anti-Tamil policy; it was a rather proactive policy to safeguard the interests of all the disadvantaged people of the country. This policy, however, was considered an anti-Tamil policy. This clearly showed the ability of Jaffna Tamils to convince the Tamils living in the rest of the country that it was a problem for the entire Tamil nation. Once again, the Tamil nationalist politicians capitalized on this educational policy to mobilize support for their own political advantage.

Anandasangaree, the leader of TULF.

In the midst of this development, Mr. Anandasangaree, the Tamil Member of Parliament from Killinochi, came forward and appealed to the government to consider Killinochi as a separate district, based on the existing local conditions. The government approved and the Tamil students from the Killinochi area benefited. In this regard, one can say that the daughter of the former LTTE leader, the late Mr. Prabaharan, was able to qualify for admittance to university from the Tamil district of Killinochi. Supporters should be highly grateful to Mr. Anandasangaree for the higher education opportunity given to their leader's daughter. While the rest of the students were forced to take part in the war, she benefited from the possibility of receiving a post-secondary education. It is obvious that the real beneficiaries of the policy were the Tamil nationalist politicians. They successfully manipulated the Tamils to mobilize and support them in the fight against the so-called discriminatory educational policy against all Tamils.

As one proceeds to explore the origin of Tamil nationalism, one will find that in the early 70's, Tamil nationalism grew in strength in the Northern provinces while the Eastern provinces showed heavy resistance to it. This could be due to the Eastern provinces' geographical proximity to the Sinhala nationalist parties as well as the large concentration of Muslims. Furthermore, one would have to say that the Tamil youths were not affected by the Standardization Policy. The large concentration of Muslims and their ability to elect their choice of leader had been a problem to the growing Tamil nationalists. Their distrust continued to grow for Muslims, and in the days of the LTTE in the 90's, Muslims were expelled from their place of habitation further south. One can certainly ask those seeking humanitarian help for Tamils: Where were you when those innocent Muslims were given 48 hours to leave their homes? Where were your humanitarian concerns?

As one looks at the following chart, it is evident that except for a few electorates, such as Mannar, Trincomalee and Batticaloa the rest of the electorates were dominated by the Sinhala nationalist parties. Among the Sinhala nationalists, the UNP was able to secure four seats and the SLFP captured three seats. This also shows that the UNP clearly appealed to Muslims with anti-Tamil sentiments.

1970 General Election

85 Mannar			
V.A. Alegacone	House	10,697	25,441
S.A. Raheem	Elephant	10,628	
N.M. Abdul Cader	Hand	513	

87 Trincomalee			
B. Neminathan	House	12,395	35,445
S.M.A. C. Jamaldeen	Hand	8,346	
R. Navaratnarajah	Elephant	5,703	
R.G.Senanayake	Bell	601	

88 Mutur

A.L. Abdul Majeed	Hand	22,727	44,176
A. Thangathurai	House	19,787	
H.D.L. Leelaratne	Ladder	18,698	
M.E.H.M. Ali	Elephant	15,018	
B.G. Sirisena	Lamp	253	

89 Kalkudah

K.W. Devanayagam	Elephant	11,205	26,670
P. Manicavasagam	House	8,420	
S. Sivagnanam	Pair of Scales	1,660	
S.S. Gabriel	Umbrella	557	
A.M. Abdul Caffoor	Hand	331	

90 Batticaloa

C. Rajadurai	House	27,661	51,524
P.R. Selvanayagam	Lamp	23,082	
A.H. Macan Markar	Elephant	17,015	
M.A.C.A. Rahuman	Hand	14,805	
S.J. Arasaratnam	Cockerel	624	
T. Francis Xavier	Pair of Scales	196	

91 Amparai

S. Somaratne	Hand	18,570	42,029
P. Dayaratne	Elephant	14,194	
Y.S. Minoris	Chair	414	

92 Paddirippu

S. Thambirajah	Elephant	13,370	28,992
S.M. Rasamanickam	House	12,723	

93 Kalmunai

M.C. Ahamed	Hand	8,779	24,693
A.R. Munsoor	Elephant	7,827	
A. Udumalebbe	House	4,960	

94 Nintavur

M.M. Mustapha	Elephant	13,481	29,718
M.I.M. Abdul Majeed	Radio	13,406	
I.H. Mohamed Cassim	Hand	556	

95 Pottuvil

M.A. Abdul Majeed	Elephant	10,610	28,282
Tharumalingam Nadarajah	Cockerel	9,335	
M.I. Abdul Jabbar	Hand	5,209	

One can also observe a new kind of candidate in the Eastern part of the Tamil region. There was a wave of Muslim candidates in most electorates appearing more frequently exhibiting their domination and influence in the region. There was also a large majority of Muslims in the interior of the Eastern province. This would make one realize that while there were Muslims representing the Tamil regions, they were either neglected by the traditional Tamil nationalists or they were not properly represented in the Tamil nationalist parties. On the contrary, Sinhala nationalists had a better representation of Muslims in their parties, in parliament and in the cabinet. Moreover, Tamil militant nationalists made it worse by driving them out of their native lands. One can also see that there were a number of Eastern provincial seats with representation for each Sinhala nationalist party, as well as some independent Muslim candidates; however, there was only one Muslim in the entire Tamil Nationalist Party.

It can also be seen that Tamil Hindu candidates from Tamil nationalist parties contested for an electorate with Muslim domination. One may not complain about this arrangement, if there were a Muslim candidate in one of the Hindu dominated northern electorates. This political formation in the East predicted very well the failure of Tamil nationalism in the East. In this regard, the breakaway of the Karuna group should not have surprised the world. It can also be argued that the East should not have been joined with the North as the aspirations of these regions were different.

The Tamil nationalists captured all of the seats in the Northern district, while gaining further seats in the East. Among the Sinhala nationalists, the UNP became the greatest winner in the election. The SLFP was totally wiped off of the scene. These election results reset the mood of the country for years to come. By this election, Tamil nationalists came to power in the Sri Lankan Parliament. Tamils became the opposition party and gained a platform to address the international community. Perhaps, here, I should mention that the Tamil issue came to the international spotlight due to the elected opposition leadership, not by the ruthless terror promoted by the LTTE.

This level of achievement by the Tamils cannot be attributed to the Tamils only. Their achievement became possible as Sinhala nationalism gave its verdict, which was a landslide victory for the United National Party. This victory for the UNP eliminated the second Sinhala nationalist party, the SLFP. The elimination of the SLFP created unintended and undesirable consequences for the Sinhala nationalists. For the first time in history, the Tamil nationalists became the official opposition in parliament; thus, the opposition status enjoyed by the Tamils was a result of growing ethno-nationalism in the country. The Tamil United Liberation Front competed in the election on the platform of the Tamil independent state. The state was called "Tamil Eelam". This was a clear mandate for them assuring that the majority of Tamils had lost their faith in the idea of a united Sri Lanka and that they wanted their leaders to fight for a separate country As the nationalist politicians became locked in this separate-states campaign, they found it difficult to negotiate with the Sinhala nationalists. As the Tamil nationalist politicians prepared to negotiate on this issue of separate states, the Tamil militants called them traitors. The Tamil nationalist politicians were now faced with a political dilemma: the separate state of Tamil Eelam had to be abandoned for a more prudent solution. As an autonomous state consisting of the North and East regions of the united Sri Lanka, they named the state Tamil Eelam. This explanation, although accepted by all the other Tamil militant groups, was not accepted by the LTTE who stood firm on their demand for a separate country. They continued to convince the Tamils that they would deliver the state through an arms struggle. In order to win the trust of the people, the LTTE launched several military assaults on many different government targets and succeeded in most of them. The Sri Lankan military plunged into a deep moral crisis and an LTTE phobia. It was some other countries, possibly India, that explained to them that the LTTE phobia was, in fact, xenophobia—the fear and hatred of foreigners. The morale of the army was boosted, the corruption within the armed forces was rooted out, and finally, foreign aid came from many sources including the Indian Navy Patrol that prevented any LTTE arms shipment.

In addition to the existing local ethnic nationalism in Sri Lanka, the growth of Tamil nationalism was possible due to the proximity to Southern India and the willingness of the former Prime Minister of India, Indira Ghandi. Her government took the initiative to train the militant groups, fund them and arm them. She was also the one who brought our problem into the international spotlight. India was the base for the Democratic Tamil nationalist leaders as well as the Tamil militants. The international community started viewing the Sri Lankan ethnic problem through the eyes of India because India had the power to show it to the world and to end the conflict.

The role of India in shaping our country's political, cultural and economic conditions was not something that started in modern times, evident in the story of Segeriya in the year 5 AD. In the year 1017 AD, the Chola king, Rajendran, from Tamil Nadu, India, defeated the Sinhala king, Mahinda, and brought the entire island under his control. Even the legendary story of Ramayana speaks of India's domination over this island. In this context, Indian involvement in training and arming Tamil militants should not surprise anyone. One also has to understand the fact that there were times in history where Tamil kings from South India had joined hands with Sinhala kings to overthrow the Tamil kingdoms. There were stories of a Tamil Pandian king from India married to a Sinhalese princess.

Tamil or Sinhalese, the political interests and diplomacy advocated were the factors that decided on the aid from Indian Kings. Indian aid was not only based on a racial relationship, it was mostly based on the political interests of India. Our Tamil militant political leaders from Sri Lanka failed to understand this fact. Moreover, they failed to understand the power of the Indian central government over and above the state government of Tamil Nadu. Lastly, the Tamil militant leaders failed to understand the consensus among Indian people as Indian interests were much greater than regional interests. If Sri Lankans believed that they could make an impact on India's national politics, they were dreaming. This would be as unrealistic as someone urinating in the ocean and believing that by doing so they would change the properties of the ocean. India is simultaneously dealing with the Sri Lankan issue, as well as that of Nepal, Tibet, Pakistan and Bangladesh. India is an ocean and it has the power to absorb and be the catalyst of change for anything and everything.

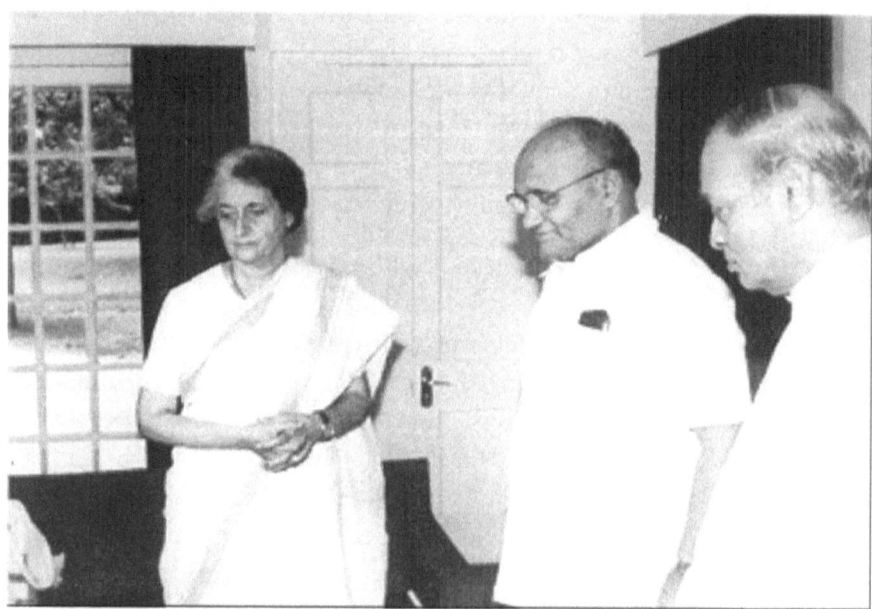

Today, Western governments cannot have an independent focused view of Sri Lanka due to their commitment to a long-lasting battle with Afghanistan coupled with the uncertainty in Pakistan. Moreover, India's economic advantage, its global skilled as well as unskilled labor market and its' large market potential would definitely keep Westerners in line with Indian policies. The last thing they would want to risk is losing India as their ally.

The interest of Western governments in the region is nothing more than the interest of the world's capitalists. The Indian subcontinent is the current interest of capitalism: India is not a regional power, it is a global power. It has a greater influence over the globe due to its comparative advantage in the economic realm. This does not mean that I would expect Tamils to accept and live with what India gives: we should, instead, focus and engage in constant political lobbying with India more than any other country.

The chapter cannot end without accusing the LTTE of assassinating democratically elected leaders. The assassinations totally eliminated one of the true and experienced political leaders who had been a negotiator. The countries that are in a position to talk are not willing to talk with someone who is labeled a terrorist.

The negotiating bodies that were created by the LTTE do not have any credibility. The subjects they raised in talk were either impossible to negotiate or irrelevant to the politics of the Tamil nation. At one point, they talked about confiscating weapons from Colonel Karuna, the leader of one breakaway faction of the LTTE in the East. As the LTTE had successfully eliminated the democratically elected Tamil nationalist leaders, they became concerned about the remaining members of the party. These members were either forced to work under the guidance of the LTTE or were met with threats to their lives. Until this point, the Tamil nationalist leaders always acted as a defense for these militant groups. With many of their members already having lost their lives, the LTTE had created their own annihilation.

In order to win back the goodwill of India and the rest of the world, we need to renounce our traditional position. We have to learn to accept and respect the minorities among us. Their political aspirations must be respected and honored. We should embrace these different groups and make sure they are represented in all our functions. Thus, Tamils should not have to travel all over the world to lobby the international community; instead, they need to focus on Indian diplomacy.

Clearly, the Tamils of Sri Lanka have a legitimate demand for a separate country. This is based on the fact that there was a Tamil government or self-rule existing prior to colonization. Secondly, the Tamils from the island systematically endured violence by the hands of the majority Sinhalese; and lastly, the majority of Tamils believe that self-rule is the only choice to enhance their social, cultural, economical and political aspirations. It should also be noted that official opposition party status in the Sri Lankan parliament along with Indian aid brought our problem to the international spotlight. Furthermore, the actions carried out by the LTTE only damaged the image of our legitimate struggle.

THE EMERGENCE OF
MILITANT NATIONALISM

As the democratic Tamil parties attempted and failed to achieve anything for more than thirty years, it was natural that it would lead to the next logical thing: an arms struggle. This was a spontaneous action initiated by desperate people, directed by Tamil nationalist politicians, carried out by experienced Tamil criminals and, lastly, funded by the Tamil capitalists.

As we have seen earlier, there were certain government policies that fueled the growing militancy amongst Tamil youth. In particular, the Standardization Policy was taken negatively by Tamil youth as it was seen as a measure aimed to curtail their academic progress. The youth, who were unable to secure places in post-secondary institutions, had no alternative choices. They had been brought up to pursue higher learning only in either medicine or engineering. Other options never existed in the minds of Jaffna Tamils.

In addition, there were not many recreational activities or other choices of entertainment, like bars and casinos, such as one would find in Western capitalist societies, Furthermore, these activities were considered socially taboo, and anyone associated with these activities could harm his or her future matrimonial prospects; and not only for himself or herself, but also for his or her siblings. Tamil youth would normally be engaged in activities organized by their local temples or churches; others would be engaged in farming and small-scale home-based economic activities. There would also be a few in every village and town active in nothing other than gathering in community centers or some common area to engage in recreational pursuits or discuss common interests. These particular youth were certainly from the middle class, with parents who were civil servants or teachers who could support them well enough to engage in leisure activities. Their parents' secure incomes provided this unproductive and unleashed group of youth with more than the necessities. They had idle minds and their idle minds became the workshop of the devil. As I was growing up, I was among this group.

We were full of unburned energy seeking for "activities". We thought we were social reformists, though the rest of the society had a very different perception of us. One can be certain that many other such groups were brewing in every village and town in Sri Lanka. The South and West had similar groups that had evolved around one social issue or another, such as unemployment, familial issues and perhaps land disputes. The youth in the North and the East had to deal with a wave of Tamil refugees landing at their door steps. This was a hot topic for many Tamil youths in the North and East. Groups that were previously engaged in some sort of gang activity and battling with the youth of neighboring villages and towns switched their attention to the issue of refugees. The blind eye shown by the Sri Lankan government on the attack of innocent civilians and its failure to protect the Tamils in the South was definitely the impetus that aided in the development of Tamil militant nationalism.

At this juncture, one has to analyze the real factors behind the race riots in our country. One could blame the LTTE entirely for the cause of violence endured by the Tamils in the South; however, some would blame it on Sinhala nationalists and declare them to be the root cause. The fact of the matter was that none of these groups had the ability to sustain the violence for very long. Furthermore, none of them had the ability to protect the interests of certain classes of Tamils residing in certain areas. There are Tamils who live in Colombo 7 who have never experienced any forms of riots or violence throughout their lives and continue to carry on their business as usual. There are businesses with large-scale investments in certain parts of the country that have never been attacked. On the contrary, ordinary Tamil small business owners were looted and killed. One really has to ask, why? This would tell us the real reason for rioting and it would also pinpoint the real culprits behind the violence. Most people killed in every riot were ordinary middle class Tamils who were engaged in small business operations, as well as Tamil civil servants.

What triggered these riots? Were they caused by an angry Sinhala mob, or were they properly organized and executed by a certain interest group in the country? What was the reason behind them? Who were the beneficiaries?

In order to investigate this, one can look at the reasoning of Tarzie Vittachi in *Emergency 58*: "This widespread fear of political, social and economic in-security is at the root of the disorders that Ceylon has been going through recently."

"At the time of Ceylon's independence there were about 7000 British nationals in the country conducting businesses. Soon after the death of D.S. Senanayake, there was a major efflux of British and capital that began. The country with the fear of lacking capital, the labor movement in the country was getting stronger and they were ready to unleash their indignation on the government. In addition to the existing turmoil the Left wing parties were after the government to nationalize the foreign owned Tea companies".

Thus, the real issue was the growing labor movements, the demand to nationalize the privately owned foreign investments and lastly, lacking capital in the market. Although, this was a mere class conflict, it was successfully diverted as a race conflict. It is interesting to see the similarities with a local example in Canada. A meat packing company in Lakeside, Alberta had a situation recently with a number of immigrant workers demanding better working conditions. Their demand had nothing to do with race; however, the majority of these immigrant workers were recent Black immigrants. As a result, the labor issue based on class conflict became a race issue. A recent attack on Indian students in Australia sets another example of capitalism's inability to resolve market conditions and how it often attempts to divert the attention of the angry masses to other issues such as race. If one argues that race was the real issue in the case of the attack on the Indian students, the question would be, why now? Indian students have existed in Australia for a long time; what changed the local condition towards them was the global economic crisis.

In the case of the Sinhala nationalist forces, they joined forces with the capitalist class to find a way to realize their political aspirations. This way out was to divert attention to the brewing emotions on the race issue. The capitalists succeeded in their attempt. They were careful enough to keep their interests intact. The evidence was the Tamil capitalist class living in Colombo 7. Even in the subsequent riots, the foreign investments in the Free Trade Zone were untouched. The Tamil families living in the secured Colombo 7 were kept safe. If the government was unable to control the rioters, how did they protect the interests of investors and the capitalist Tamils? The idea of rioting was to divert the attention of the innocent people of Sri Lanka who would take up arms and kill each other to serve the interest of the capitalists.

As anger grew among the Tamil youth, along with their natural affinity for guns, they were driven to secure arms. Some started making their own bombs and seriously injured themselves. Others executed emotionally driven attacks on government targets, such as buses and trains. There were a few others secretly planning large-scale plots.

In order to understand the emergence of militancy among young people, I should share a portion of my own story with you in the proceeding paragraph; however, I will further discuss the development of Tamil militancy for now. As we all know, the idea of militancy is usually associated with the younger generation. In the history of Tamil nationalism, nothing affected the Tamil youth until the advent of an educational policy called "Standardization." The fear of possibly not being able to pursue post-secondary studies, coupled with the pressure to compete with those who had a greater chance even with lower grades, sparked an angry group of young people lining up for a rebellion against the government.

In the midst of this development there was a second group, the English-educated civil servants protesting against the government language policy, a policy that required Tamil staff to learn Sinhala in order to get promoted. The idea of native language "Suyabazzawa" originated from the fact that the majority of the population were unable to read, write or even speak English. Although, the government policies emanated from the idea of being proactive to protect and serve the common people living in rural villages, it backfired on the basis of minority interest; particularly, the interests of Tamil students in Jaffna with aspirations for higher education, and the well-being of most of the Jaffna middle class. The English-educated Tamil civil servants faced the mental distress of having to pass a Sinhala proficiency test. The formation of student organizations and of Tamil civil servants became a spontaneous amalgamation under the circumstances.

Thus, the growth of militancy among Tamil youth was fueled by a failed government's educational policy. While civil servants were staging their protest against the Sinhala requirement for promotion, the Tamil Manavar Peravai (Tamil Students League) and the Tamil Elaingyar Peravai (Tamil Youth League) became the most radical groups. The function of the Tamil nationalist politicians was to coordinate these two groups and manipulate them to achieve their political goal. However, there were some from the student bodies and some from the Tamil Civil Servants Association that became highly interested not only in playing the role of contributors, but also of playing the role of manipulators. For example, one of the leaders, Mr. Mavai Senathirajah from the Elaingyar Peravai currently, in the Tamil Nationalist Party serving the Tamil National Alliance. The second most important contribution came from the Tamil civil servants. Mr. Eelaventhan, a prominent member in the Tamil nationalist movement and also a former Member of Parliament from the Tamil National Alliance, came from the civil servants' camp. So far, one can see that the combination of vehement Tamil youth groups along with intellectuals from the civil service together had the potency to organize more than a civil protest. Howbeit, the involvement of youth in the civil protests often ended in violence.

As the law enforcement officials began searching for the trouble-makers, the youth had to find some protection. This invited the Tamil criminals to offer their services to the Tamil nationalist movement. They rendered these services in the form of protecting and sheltering the young Tamil militant nationalists who were wanted by the Sri Lankan government for their alleged involvement in criminal activities. Figures like Kuttimani and Chetti came to the aid of the wanted youth by transporting them to Tamil Nadu, India. Once again, Tamil criminals also wanted to have dual roles; that is, while contributing to the criminal aspect of Tamil nationalism, they, too, desired political leadership. Traditional Tamil nationalist parties could not accept a convicted criminal as a politician. So, as the political parties continued to neglect criminals, despite their contributions, the Tamil criminals started their own political movement. The New Tamil Tigers was born as Chetti and Kannadi Pathmanathan broke out of Annurajapura prison in the early 70's. The LTTE was conceived in the womb of Tamil criminals. Its growth took place in the hands of several foster parents and every time the child suffered with difficulties, it was safely transported to Tamil Nadu, India. Tamil Nadu was the incubator for this weak child.

The Tamil criminal gang called the New Tamil Tigers started robbing several cooperative banks, private pawn shops and some national banks. The money was lavishly spent on women, alcohol, travel and all other kinds of entertainment. This group of criminals joined with some political radicals like Prabaharan and staged several murders and murder attempts. (A list of these murder victims can be found at www.spur.asn.au):

Local and National political leaders

1.	A T Duraiyappah	Mayor for Jaffna
2.	A Thiagarajah	MP for Vadokoddai who later joined the UNP
3.	K T Pulendran	UNP Organiser for Vavunia
4.	A J Rajasooriar	UNP Organiser in Jaffna
5.	Mala Ramachandran	UNP MMC for Baticaloa
6.	V Dharmalingam	Ex TULF MP for Manipay and Father of D Siddharthan, Leader of PLOTE
7.	Alakasunderam	TULF MP for Kopay
8.	Gnanachandiram	District Judge, Point Pedro and Government Agent, Mullativu

9.	C. E Anandarajah	Principal, St Jones College, Jaffna.
10.	B K Thambipillai	President, Citizens Cimmittee
11.	P Kirubakaran	Primary Court Judge
12.	Kathiramalai	Sarvodaya Leader
13.	Vignarajah	Assistant Government Agent, Samanturai
14.	Anthonimuttu	Government Agent, Baticaloa
15.	S S Jeganathan	Assistant Government Agent, Baticaloa
16.	Sinnadurai	Assistant Government Agent, Trincomalee
17.	M E Kandasamy	Principal, Palugamam Maha Vidyalaya
18.	S Siththamparanathan	Principal, Vigneswara Vidyalaya, Trincomalee
19.	S Wijayanadan	Distric Secretary, Ceylon Communist Party
20.	Velmurugu Master	TULF Organiser and Citizens Committee Member, Kalmunai
21.	Rev. Father Chandra Fernando	President, Citizens Committee, Batticaloa
22.	Rajjshankar	President, Citizens Committee, Tennamarachchi
23.	S Sambandamoorthy	Ex TULF Chairman, District Development Council, Batticaloa
24.	V M Panchalingam	Government Agent, Jaffna
25.	K Pulendran	Assistant Government Agent, Kopay
26.	A Amirthalingam	TULF Leader and National List MP
27.	V Yogeshwaran	Ex TULF MP for Jaffna

28.	Dr (Mrs) Rajini Thiranagama	Lecturer in Anatomy at the Jaffna University and co-author of the "Broken Palmyrah" (21 Sptember 1989)
29.	Ganeshalingam	Ex EPRLF Provincial Minister for North and East
30.	Sam Thambimuttu	EPRLF MP
31.	Mrs Thambimuttu	Wife of EPRLF MP
32.	V Yogasangari	EPRLF MP in Madras
33.	A Thangadurai	TULF MP for Trincomalee
34.	Mrs Sarojini Yogeshwaran	TULF Mayoress for Jaffna
35.	Pon Sivapalan	TULF Mayor of Jaffna
36.	Canagasabai Rajathurai	EPDF Member for Jaffna
37.	Veerahaththy Gunaratnam	PLOTE member of the Pachchilaipalli Pradheshiya Sabha (PS) in Jaffna (5 May 1999)
38.	Razick,	Supremo of the EPRLF's armed wing (30 May 1999)
39.	Dr Neelan Thiruchelvam	Leader of TULF (29 July 1999)
40.	N. Manickathasan	Vice President of PLOTE (Tamil Political party working with the Sri Lankan Government)
41.	Kumar Ponnambalam	President of All Ceylon Tamil Congress (5 Jan 2000)
42.	Vadivelu Vijeyaratnam	Point Pedro Urban Council Chairman (14 Jan 2000)
43.	Anton Sivalingam	EPDP's Municipal Council members in Jaffna (1 March 2000)

44.	Kanapathipillai Navaratnarajah	TELO member of Arayampathi, Batticaloa - on 7 June 2000
45.	Rajan Sathiyamoorthy	Tamil National Alliance parliamentary candidate Rajan Sathiyamoorthy was killed by LTTE Tamil Tiger Terrorists on 30 March 2004.
46.	Hon. Lakshman Kadirgamar	(Foreign Minister in Sri Lanka) 12 August 2005 - Read full details in Special Web Edition
47.	Kethishwaran Loganathan	(54) Deputy Secretary General of Sri Lanka Peace Secratariat, SCOOP (12 August 2006)
48.	T Maheshwaran	Former Minister shot dead on 01 January 2008 (New Years day)
49.	Minister D M Dissanayake	LTTE Tamil Tigers Assassinate Minister D M Dissanayake; 12 people Injured; Another Person killed (03 January 2008)
50.	K Sivanesan	Jaffna TNA MP K. Sivanesan killed in an accidental explosion of a LTTE Tamil Tiger Claymore mine in the LTTE held area (05 March 2008).
51.	Minister Jeyaraj Fernandopulle	LTTE Tamil Tiger Terrorist's Suicide Bomb Attack killing Minister Jeyaraj Fernandopulle and 12 civilians (06 April 2008)
52.	Rev. Father M. X. Karunaratnam,	Chairman of the North East Secretariat on Human Rights (NESOHR), a Catholic priest attached to the Jaffna diocese (20 April 2008)

53.	Ms. Maheswary Velautham	Attorney –at-law and advisor to the Minister of Social Services and Social Welfare, Douglas Devananda shot dead by the LTTE Tamil Tiger terrorists on 13 May 2008 (Details in EPDP).

Political radicals, such as the late Mr. Prabaharan, started questioning the practices of Chetti and others. Subsequently, he murdered people one by one and eventually took full control of the group. While the LTTE was establishing itself and carrying out several attacks, there were a number of other groups brewing in the North and East Tamil regions. Some of them were coordinated by the LTTE and some joined the LTTE, while others started functioning independently. In the same way, the LTTE had gone through various stages and gathered some new members while ejecting those that disagreed or questioned them. Most of those that disagreed with Prabaharan were murdered in a subtle manner. Only a few were lucky enough to escape death.

I was in the midst of a small new gang of youth planning on taking some action. This was ironic because I ended up meeting some of my father's former political enemies. One of them was the person who actually planted the bomb at our house. He even showed me how he did it.

We all were united for one thing, which was to stage violent protests on behalf of refugees; we were not driven by any political ideology or any definite plan for militancy. The nearest police station was the target, Ravi suggested. Everyone agreed, but I had a problem with this. My problem was that none of us had ever had any weapons training except for one named Kumar who was from the Sri Lankan Air force. (Ravi and Kumar both died in India.) There was a very dedicated supporter of my father named "Motti"; whom we approached for weapons. The only kind of weapon that he could possibly find for us were regular shotguns. These were used on large farms in the jungle to keep wildlife away and on some occasions, they were used for hunting.

Once our hardware became available, we needed to find some way to operate them effectively. We looked for a trainer. As we searched, we met a person named "Thiru" who had come from the United Kingdom on holidays to attend the local temple celebration. He convinced us that he was a trainer for the Sinhala youth during the 70's, and that he could provide some training for us in the South. He asked us to meet him in Colombo. We had no money to travel, but I had a wrist watch that could be traded for train tickets. Mr. Thiru picked us up at the Colombo train station and drove us to a house in Colombo City adjacent to a large lake. The property was very big and covered by large trees. He instructed us to tell the lady of the house that we were there to board a ship. We pretended that Thiru was finding us employment on a shipping liner. The lady of the house was Sinhalese and she was very kind to us and looked after our meals and lodging. Thiru promised to return to us the following day to commence the training. He never showed up. Days became weeks, and still there was no sign of him. During our stay, it was customary for us to wake up every morning and begin our daily physical training: we had some knowledge of martial arts. Having observed us for days and weeks, the lady became curious about our activities and asked if we were actually there for employment on a shipping liner. Our answer was, "yes".

As we lost hope of Thiru ever showing up, we decided to thank to the lady of the house and pack our bags to return to Jaffna. We never questioned the relationship of that lady to Thiru; however, the lady did look after us as though we were family. The money we had was only enough to purchase one platform ticket. So, we bought one ticket and sent Ravi to the station. Ravi came to the side of the steel wired fence and handed out the same ticket to me. I entered the station and handed the ticket over to the next person, Sami. The story of this person Sami is very interesting, more so than any one of us in the group. Sami was my classmate during my high school days and later he went and joined a "Hare Rama Hare Krishna" missionary in Colombo. However, his dedication to God was terminated as I convinced him to join our group for the liberation of the Tamils.

Reaching Jaffna, we decided to rethink our plan of attack on the police station. I suggested that we contact a friend of mine who was highly experienced in these areas. My friend's name was Santhathyar. He was the fifth person accused in Alfred Durayappah's murder case, and clearly highly active in these affairs. I came to know him from his visits to my father. It was a unanimous decision to write to him. As we expected, he came to our place and we all met him in a local village temple. It took a couple of meetings before we concluded that we would work together.

I traveled with Santhathyar to Vavuniya and met Mr. Uma Maheswaran and Mr. Paranthan Rajan. The latter had left the PLOTE in the early 90's to start his own militant group and Maheswaran was the former General Secretary of the LTTE. Previous to his expulsion, Maheswaran had been warned about his personal conduct—he had been accused of having an illegitimate sexual relationship with his relative, Urmela—amongst other things. He was later expelled from the LTTE by the late Mr. Prabaharan. Having lived for some time in the United Kingdom, he returned to Sri Lanka to create a new organization. At the time of this meeting, he was a wanted man in Sri Lanka.

There was a small group of people associated with us; however, we were growing in numbers. I was assigned to work with Santhathyar, and to look after the administration and organizational aspect of the group. My fellow members joined the militant wing of the group. The first meeting was held in Trincomalee, in the eastern province; this was where our political bureau was formed. Uma Maheswaran assumed the role of General Secretary, Santhathyar was appointed as Organizational Secretary and I was appointed as Administrative Secretary. The organization was named the PLOTE (Peoples Liberation Organization of Tamil Eelam). We agreed that our flag would be black and red with a yellow star in the top right corner. District organizers were appointed. The PLOTE launched its first attack on a police station in the Northern district and recovered all of its weapons. Following this, the bank in Killinochi was emptied in the middle of the night. Because the organization had carried off a successful attack on the police station, it became attractive to many Tamil youths. The growth of this organization would certainly have been envied by the late Mr. Prabaharan.

There was also a newspaper that we printed called, "New Path", which was printed in Jaffna by a printing press called Chittira Press. At this point I would like to say that one of the victims of LTTE brutality was the late Mr. C.E. Anandarajah, who was my teacher and principal during the 1980's. I remember him buying 25 Christmas cards published by the PLOTE entitled, "Jesus Wanted".

One fine morning, one of our leaders named Sundaram was gunned down at the press by Charles Antony, an LTTE militant whose name was given to Prabaharan's son. The press was supposed to be a place for me to sit with Sundaram and do a proofreading of the monthly newspaper. As I did not show up for the proofreading session, my own organization started to think that I was behind the murder of Mr. Sundaram and that I had become an agent for the LTTE. Consequently, I became wanted by three fronts: the Sri Lankan Army, the LTTE and the PLOTE.

I clearly understand now that this was the nature of these kinds of organizations; however, at that time, I was very lost and needed a way out of Sri Lanka. I searched my father's old day planners and found the address of a member of the Legislative Assembly in neighboring Tamil Nadu, India. His name was Chandran Jeyabalan and he was from the DMK party for T. Nagar, Chennai. I did not have any illegal form of transportation because of my strained relationship with the organization, so I had to go through the regular channel--traveling through Colombo and then flying. The journey was somewhat risky, but I had no other alternatives. As I went through immigration, I was stopped and told that I could not proceed. The Sri Lankan Immigration Officer stamped on the eleventh page of my passport, "The above endorsement is hereby cancelled as the holder is not proceeding on his Journey". I tried to stay calm! I was told to take a seat and wait. A few hours later I was put on the next flight with no questions asked. Until this day, I do not know why I was held at the airport.

Comrade Suntharam

The late Mr. Sundaram, assassinated by the LTTE in the early 80's

Finally, when I landed in Madras (presently Chennai) I was informed that Mr. Chandran Jeyabalan had passed away a couple of years ago. The house was occupied by the landlord and the only person that was there to receive me was the youngest member of the family, Ragu, who was twelve years old. He took pity on me and insisted that I stay there. I had no other choice but to take him up on this fortunate offer. I quietly sat in the living room with my small bag beside me. I only had one thousand five-hundred Indian rupees in my pocket. This would have only given me about three months of the cheapest accommodation. Within this time, I planned to contact my father, who was employed as a study organizer in a co-operative college in Lusaka, Zambia. The rest of the family came home one by one, and they quickly accommodated me in the front room of the house.

I enjoyed a very comfortable life there. As I was establishing myself, I often visited a place called Pondy Bazaar, the same place where the leaders of the LTTE, Mr. Prabaharan and Rahaven spotted Uma Maheswaran along with Jotheswaran and shot at them. They were arrested on the spot and Maheswaran was arrested in Kommunipoondi in Andhra Pradesh.

Having ceased my short-lived rebel life, I had to find new places and new faces to protect myself. Following the shootout between these warring factions, the Tamil Nadu police had intensified their search for Sri Lankan Tamil youth in Madras. It so happened, that the uncle of Ragu was appointed as the investigating officer in Madras and he would be coming to stay for a time at the same house I was residing in. Since I had previously shared my story with the family, they made arrangements to shift me from Madras to Bangalore along with their older son, Ravi.

I was protected and looked after by this family even during a time that I was battling Liver Disease. Sadly, Ragu's mother, who took care of me during my illness and had sheltered and protected me from all sorts of dangers including a possible interrogation by her brother, passed away from cancer in the late 90's. Ragu, her son who had so willingly helped me as a young boy, had become a computer programmer and is now residing in the United States. Thankfully, I was able to see Ragu's mother again before her death during a visit she paid me after I moved to Canada. I have since made two trips to Madras and have visited the rest of the family. Ravi is now settled in Bangalore and is practicing real estate. My connection to this family was beyond anything I could have ever imagined: perhaps, it was a connection that I had in my past life.

While I was residing in India, there were two youths murdered in my village of Alaveddy. They were considered close allies or informants to the LTTE. On the belief that they were the informants for the murder of the late Mr. Sundaram at the Jaffna printing press, the PLOTE executed them. One of them was Iryaikumaran, a close relative of mine and a long-term member of the Tamil Ilanyar Peravai. Despite the fact that he was a long-time opponent of my father's political views, he became close to me during my involvement with the PLOTE: we occasionally met and talked. The second person was Umaikumaran, a very close friend of Iryaikumaran. Umaikumaran was highly active with the Kuttimani TELO, and we became close in later days. He was also part of the group that planted a bomb on our house. The fact that I was close to them and close to Raghavan's brother (Raghavan was a relative of mine on my wife's side), made the PLOTE think that I was spying and that I informed the LTTE of the murder of Mr. Sundaram. I was blamed for the murder of the late Mr. Sundaram and the two youth from my village. I had made the best of enemies that one could ever dream of. In the midst of all this, there was a good possibility that the government was looking for me because of documents obtained from the press or the information given to them by my political enemies. To this day I receive threats from people accusing me of murdering the two youth from my village. Here is one such message:

Velupillai commented on your wall:

"I am [sic] ashamed and disgusted when i [sic] came to know that you are stupid son of the illustrious father V.P. You are the one who murdered the innocent two youngsters in your home town. You are talking about the brutality of our freedom fighters."

These kinds of threats are techniques to silence those who speak against the Tamil nationalists. However, there are some who get challenged by these kinds of emails. As you see, I am one of them.

This episode of mine was nothing compared to what many others went through in the name of Tamil militancy. Unlike my story, most did not escape from the cruelty of Tamil militancy. There was a prominent member of the PLOTE named Sivanesan, who protected and sheltered Maheswaran from the LTTE and was also brutally beaten to death by Maheswaran. Most of our political bureau members were murdered in a most cruel fashion because of the internal conflict within the organization. Santhayiyar was murdered by the organization. Ravi, from my village had to escape from the PLOTE camp using an ambulance. In the process, even Uma Maheswaran was killed by his very close associates. Murder had become a disease that was inherited from the root of the organization. There were days when I would feel guilty for leaving my fellow comrades behind; however, the needless killing of our own people made me praise my wisdom.

Apart from the killing of fellow militants, there were a number of civilians that were killed for questioning or disputing them. The case of Mr. Murugesu Dharmarajan starts with his merchant navy training studies and graduation in Colombo, Sri Lanka. As he planned to search for employment, he met with opposition from his mother. During his stay in his native town of Killinochi, he found employment with the Ceylon Transport Board. He worked as a conductor for the bus route from Colombo to Killinochi: this classified him as a person of interest to the LTTE. The LTTE approached him to transport some parcels with undisclosed items. His disagreement to carry out their order made him an enemy. On one occasion, he purchased some locks for his residence in Killinochi and transported them on a company bus. The LTTE caught him and accused him of transporting items without paying the due freight charges. He was taken into custody and interrogated; the LTTE found him guilty for transporting items on a Sri Lankan public transportation vehicle without paying the charges. The interesting point here was that the LTTE had charged someone for a violation that occurred on the property of the Sri Lankan government. Secondly, the punishment for transporting items without a charge was stoning. He was brought to a public place and tied to a lamp post while a tractor-load of stones was brought to the site. The LTTE carders stood along the sidelines and began stoning him. The dead body of this young employee of the Ceylon Transport Board was left there for public viewing.

The case of "Palali" Sivarajah is another example of the LTTE's brutality in the North. Palali refers to a town in the KKS electorate. Since Sivarajah was born and brought up in this town, he was popularly known to others by his town's name followed by his first name. Palali was a bastion of Tamil nationalism and despite this general political trend, "Palali" Sivarajah was a dedicated Communist Party member. He was very close to my father, V. Ponnamapalam and the rest of my family. "Palali" Sivarajah was taken away by the LTTE for a "small talk" while in the midst of dining with his family. The LTTE carders took him and never released any information to his family. His wife went to inquire about her husband every day for months and she was always told to come back the following day. Having led her on for months over this issue, The LTTE finally told her that he had been executed on the same night he was apprehended.

The brutality against the innocent Tamil civilians was not only a characteristic of the LTTE, but it is endemic to every Tamil militant group. There was a community activist and a Communist Party member in Alaveddy named Jeyakumar who had condemned the reckless driving of the TELO (Tamil Eelam Liberation Organization), which had caused the death of a child. He was taken to their court of law and beaten with a sand-filled pipe. His murderers were TELO carders.

The very first person who became a victim of this disease of violence was Mr. Patkunam. He was a member of the LTTE who had questioned the leadership of Mr. Prabaharan in the early 70's. Even Raghavan, who fought alongside the late Mr. Prabaharan in Pondy Bazaar, India and was a close associate of Prabaharan from the days of Alfred's murder in the early 70's, had to flee from the LTTE.

The terror, brutality, dictatorship and thirst for blood was not only an ascribed value of the LTTE, it had been prevalent in every militant Tamil organization. The degree of these characteristics varied but definitely existed in all. There was not a single organization that had a clear understanding of the issue that they thought they were fighting for. Even to this present day, most of the fighters are bound emotionally by the idea of "Tamils". In the minds of most Tamil nationalists, "Tamils" refers to all Tamils excluding Muslims, hill country Tamils and the outcasts.

One should understand the fact that the Tamil nationalists are of the upper caste and upper class, and are highly educated members of Sri Lankan society. The agenda of these people is very different from those who appear before the public and stage illegal road blocks during demonstrations. We have seen this group of emotionally-driven Tamil people constantly around nationalist stages since the independence from Britain. The Tamil militants were undoubtedly the best of soldiers in terms of their commitment to die for their leader more than the actual cause. There are around 33 militant Tamil groups that have emerged over the years. This is a clear piece of evidence that there were many different voices representing Tamil society.

In the midst of all these different voices, the LTTE was claiming sole representation. It was the idea of sole representation that triggered attacks on every other political group. The purpose of their campaign was to annihilate these groups. Some of them faded by themselves or amalgamated with the major groups. These major organizations, of course, were the LTTE, the PLOTE, the TELO, the EPRLF, and the EROS. Due to internal conflict among these groups, there were a number of new ones started by those who left these organizations. Although, some of them still exist in small numbers, most of them are either doing some sort of illegal business to survive or have evolved as an organization for debate and discussion and for criticizing all groups but, not their own.

In the case of the LTTE, however, all rebellious factions within the organization have been brutally crushed, except for Colonel Karuna. There are a number of reasons for his survival. The most prominent one is the fact that he is from the Eastern region of the conflict and focuses on the cause of regional nationalism. The LTTE was very concerned about handling him militarily. They tried to play the usual subtle games with him, which was a game he had played for more than twenty years and had mastered every move. He survived and tried to stand alone as a unit. This became difficult as the LTTE was infiltrating the Eastern region on a daily basis. He could not fight enemies on two fronts and was forced to work out a deal with one of his enemies. He had to embrace the inevitable coalition with the very government against which he had plotted and fought for more than twenty years. This coalition can be considered as one of the factors for the downfall of the LTTE.

Former EPRLF Leader, the late Mr. Patmanapa, killed by the LTTE.

On June 6 2009, the day of mourning for the late Mr. Sivakumaran was announced. He was the first one to have committed suicide during the Tamil militancy of the early 70's. He was partly a product of misconception as the government introduced the Standardization Policy. His misconception was further fueled by nationalist politicians. He can be considered as the founder of the Tamil suicide mission. If Tamil repatriates were to ever start mourning for those who were killed by the militant Tamil nationalists, every day would have to be declared as a day of mourning.

The LTTE had a strategic plan of action to remove their competition. The LTTE managed to convince the leaders of the TELO, the EPRLF, and the EROS to make a peace accord with them based on the belief that they would jointly work to gain the political support of the Tamils. They joined with the LTTE in India, posed for photographs and even gave a joint press conference; but, none of their aspirations were realized. They were betrayed by the LTTE: all of these leaders, except for the leader of the EROS, were murdered one by one by the late Mr. Prabaharan. The EROS leader was forced to join the LTTE. He is believed to have survived and to have been taken into custody by the Sri Lankan forces in the "Wanni Operation".

The act of killing these leaders was not only a betrayal of the trust of their followers; it succeeded in annihilating any possible alternate voice. This act of betrayal should be considered as treason to the Tamil Nation. If one had to explain this in the language of the LTTE, Prabaharan and his leadership was the real traitor to the Tamil cause because they effectively organized, then systematically terminated all of the other political voices among Tamils and took the leadership of the Tamils toward destruction, defeat and humiliation.

"One by one, the TELO, PLOTE and EPRLF were devoured by the LTTE, which was determined to establish its hegemony as the 'sole representative' of the Tamil people. Even as other groups, led by the TULF were using India's good offices to press Colombo for a framework that would devolve powers to the Tamils and allow for a merger of the Northern and Eastern provinces that could constitute a Tamil homeland, the LTTE was disdainful of these parleys" (Hindu Opinion: April 24, 2009).

Now, they have issued a call to "silence the guns". The real mockery in this announcement was that the repatriate Tamils, who continue to live under an illusion, totally reject this call. They continue to raise the LTTE flag and pretend that the war is still going on. In the midst of this emotional drama, there are a few others engaged in a kind of propaganda that there are still five thousand LTTE fighters on the ground and that they are in need of financial support. Unfortunately, there are still many vulnerable Tamils that continue to feel sympathy for these vultures and are even willing to offer them cash. These vultures continue to prey on the dead bodies lying in the deserted hot soil of our motherland.

Our people cannot liberate themselves unless they free themselves from the illusions they hold. The end of the LTTE would not completely end the arms struggle; however, the intensity of its actions and attacks would certainly diminish. The vehemence that prevails among the people against being humiliated and left without any legitimate political solutions by the Sri Lankan government would certainly create the birth of a new political movement. The direction it would take, in terms of how to carry out the fight, is yet to be seen.

The Dead body of Velupillai Prabhakaran displayed by the Army.

The LTTE's shortsighted and adventurist positions have cost the Tamil ethnic cause dearly even as valuable time has been lost in the failure to consolidate the gains achieved through political negotiations.

There is nothing wrong with the arms struggle, but its role in our freedom fight should only be a part of it: it cannot become the soul of our battle for freedom. A political party that was not associated with the arms struggle should have existed. The goal of the arms struggle should only have been focused on putting military pressure on the Sri Lankan government while letting the political parties negotiate with the government independently. Appealing to the international community should only have been done through those parties, and not at all by the militant groups. The political greed of the LTTE has resulted in what we have been recently seeing. Their being our sole representation in our freedom fight has resulted in bankrupting the entire objective of our struggle. Its defeat and destruction is the sole responsibility of the LTTE and the real culprits of this destruction are the members of the Tamil diaspora.

The Expansion of Transnationalism

Tamil repatriates, who migrated to the West, actively organized their cultural organizations for the sake of socializing and exhibiting their cultural values to others, particularly to Westerners. In the process, they became local community leaders who carried out the agenda of providing cultural events and becoming spokespeople for the community. They found these activities to be a leisurely and an effective way to relax their minds from their daily routines.

During the 1980's there were a number of Tamil physicians in the U.S. that were totally engaged in this type of leisure work in attempts to promote their social statuses. There was even a point in time when one Tamil poet, for cash incentives, began penning encomiums of praise for these doctors. The recipients of this acclaim were often compared with one another. These intellectuals soon became rivals and started contributing to different militant Tamil groups stationed in India. They justified and attributed their contributions as some type of political ideology. In fact, their monetary contributions were given merely on the basis of their personal rivalry in local politics. This shows the leaders' quest to attain a similar social class or status to that which was even once enjoyed by ancient Tamil royalty. During my stay in Beverly Hills, California in 1984, I was able to observe this kind of rivalry among the Tamil doctors.

They became closely connected with Tamil nationalist politicians in Sri Lanka while having their secret monetary contributions directed to the Tamil militant groups stationed in Tamil Nadu, India. Consequently, as the rivalry of local politicians became apparent, each started his own association and became the president of that association. On a recent radio broadcast of CBC Radio One's, "Writers and Company", The writer declared that "I lead but no followers." This, too, is the case among Tamil repatriates. They all like to lead but not follow. These self-appointed, highly-educated professionals were able to portray themselves as the leaders of their community by circulating and making connections with top ranking Western political leaders. For Western political leaders, these so-called community leaders seemed like representatives of a block of Tamil votes. The large sum of money at their disposal, along with the association of relatives whom they had helped to migrate to the Western world, jointly helped them to stage a spectacular reception for the Western politicians. Most of these leaders, being doctors with plentiful amounts of money and homes in highly reputable neighborhoods, attracted Bollywood movie stars to their homes. This led to a new positive development in their search for leadership. The local Tamils desired to visit these homes in order to have a close view of these celebrities.

Tamil Community leaders, in the Western world, started searching for power and status in their birthplace. They became aware of the fact that they should associate themselves with the winning party. The winning party seemed to be the LTTE, so they decided to render their support to the LTTE. Some of them flew to Sri Lanka and had their photos taken with the late Mr. V. Prabaharan, knowing that displaying such a photo in their living rooms would certainly demonstrate that they were "pure" Tamils with authority in the local Tamil community. This accreditation enabled the individual to decide on and pronounce who was a traitor and who was a loyal member. While the LTTE embarked on commercializing their nationalistic politics, the business-minded Tamil repatriates in the Western world seized this golden opportunity for politicizing their commercial interests. The intellectual-based Tamil repatriates viewed this imported Tamil nationalism as a means of increasing their social statuses.

In the midst of all these developments, some others felt it was too political to take part in. Furthermore, Tamil repatriates from India had either no interest or less interest in Sri Lankan Tamil politics. As a result of this development among repatriated Tamils, there were several Tamil groups with different ambitions that had taken different directions.

Overall, this idea of Tamil nationalism beyond Sri Lanka's political border became an idea that would yield mutual benefits for both parties. By "both parties", I am referring to the LTTE militant leadership stationed in Sri Lanka and the repatriates in the Western world. Once again, the term "repatriates" includes three different groups, namely, middle class Tamil intellectuals with political aspirations, small business owners seeking to create a unified Tamil market and, lastly, the organized Tamil criminal gangs who served to link the LTTE in Sri Lanka with the above two groups.

It is not surprising to see that the organization followed the same pattern as it did in Sri Lanka. The Tamil criminals were always protected by the Tamil middle class intellectuals who acted as their legal counsel. As we saw in an earlier chapter, the Tamil nationalist politicians were mostly lawyers by profession; most of them had been educated in the West and served on the Queen's Council. Their only aspiration was to attain higher political statuses. The work of small business owners, the future Tamil capitalists, was to provide the necessary funding for the growth of nationalism, including covering any legal costs and other related expenses with the expectation of a higher yield in the future. Oftentimes, the growing Tamil capitalists and Tamil criminals would seek the counsel of these lawyers and, therefore, were obliged to offer their support to the Tamil nationalist politicians. In addition to the existing package of Tamil nationalist criminal lawyers and criminals, a new forceful group emerged as a result of a bad government policy. This new group was comprised of high school students who had been negatively affected by the Standardization Policy adopted by the Sri Lankan government.

Frustrated youth, with immense energy and an excitement for thrills and adventure, had entered the scene of Tamil nationalist politics. This advent of Tamil youth in the arena of politics took the struggle to the next level. This stage of politics has proven to be the most dangerous one due to the fact that it has begun to spread to many different places in a coordinated fashion. This kind of development is currently taking shape in North America where the growth of this movement is being facilitated by advanced technologies, such as the internet. As I have already pointed out, the association of criminals and Tamil nationalist politicians who were lawyers by profession had mutual benefits.

As this idea of Tamil nationalism began to emerge among repatriates, it found fertile ground in major cities in the Western world. Liberal policies of the West, coupled with multiculturalism and Human Rights laws, enabled the repatriates to disguise their political agenda and evolve as a cultural organization. There are a number of organizations and officials that sprang up with the blessing of the LTTE in Sri Lanka. In the midst of all this, they came to the realization that associating business with the god and goddess would be the most lucrative thing to do. Hence, they undertook the adventure of performing "Pooja" to these supernatural forces and, accordingly, filled their pockets: whatever spilled out of their pockets would reach the LTTE. The LTTE had to accept and live with this arrangement because for the LTTE, something is always better than nothing.

There was an organization called the Canada Tamil Sangam that was inaugurated in Ottawa in the mid 80's. It was an association that was initially started to function as a cultural organization meant to celebrate Tamil Hindu as well as Christian events. This is one of the organizations that Canada has designated as a cultural, linguistic and charitable organization. As an example, Canada Tamil Sangam of Ottawa emerged as a cultural organization consisting of Sri Lankan Tamils as well as Indian Tamils and went through the same dynamic changes illustrated above. The Tamil nationalist program along with a personal greed for power instigated a power struggle between the groups that espouse Sri Lankan Tamil nationalist politics and the groups with a purely cultural interest. There was a third group that deviated from Tamil nationalism headed by the LTTE that chose to organize itself as a cultural group and named itself the Tamil Eelam Cultural Heritage Organization. This organization gave a cultural performance for a Canada Day celebration at Parliament Hill.

Formation, division and, finally, sustainability of these various organizations largely depended on their financial resources. Once again, the

LTTE-backed organizations outperformed others through legitimate as well as illegitimate fundraising activities. Resourceful organizations with the backing of the LTTE started seeking intellectuals to represent them and to carry out their political agenda in the Western world. The development of Tamil nationalism appeals to those Tamil repatriates who have achieved their academic as well as financial positions but lack their desired social status. A prominent scholar in Ottawa became highly interested in this golden opportunity and departed on his journey to possess the leadership position. He first visited Wanni and received a personal blessing from Prabaharan, and then he moved on to Toronto to secure the support of Tamils. Despite his efforts and the direct instruction of the late Mr. V. Prabaharan to support him, he lost the election in Markham.

The Canada Tamil Sangam was a gathering of Tamils from Sri Lanka and Tamil Nadu, India along with a very few recent refugees, including myself. I was not an active participant but an observer in the crowd. There were a few things that I was able to observe: the first thing that was evident was the urge of individuals to promote themselves and, secondly, some liked to gather secretively with a small circle of friends in order to operate apart from the larger organization. It was like organizing a plot against one's own members. This was obvious in the case of the Indian Tamil leadership in the organization. There were similar stories in Toronto, where large numbers of LTTE supporters entered as members during the election and took control over the organizations. Sadly, this was the case with even the temple administration: there was a highly reputable and prominent Hindu priest who was expelled from his temple, which was then taken over by the LTTE. This irreverent and malicious act on the part of the LTTE was a great offense to the god and goddess.

Toronto, Canada and London, England, both with respectively large Tamil repatriate populations, evolved as major centers for fundraising.

A Tamil political cultural event in Canada: Pongu Thamil.

The development of Tamil nationalism among repatriated Tamils in major Western cities has facilitated commerce among them and has created an economic system that is largely different from the Western economy. A typical example is Chettu. Chettu is a system that existed in the absence of the modern banking system that was designed to encourage savings and lending based on verbal contracts and mere trust. In this system of Chettu, members would pool their equal contributions of money every month and open it for the other members to claim the entire portion. When there were more people claiming the money, they had to discount a portion of the large sum. Whoever discounted the highest amount became the winner in the process. The discounted amount was the amount that the other members saved. Participants in less need of cash would prefer to earn more by being the last person to withdraw the funds. Money pooling gave more earnings to the wealthy and also gave an opportunity to the needy to have access to immediate cash. The discounted amount was the interest that the needy paid for borrowing. If an individual member was experiencing real financial difficulties coupled with an inability to sacrifice a large amount, then the individual could appeal to the rest of the group not to demand the discounted portion. In a market with more needy people, interest would be high; in other words, the most impoverished members would have to sacrifice a much higher portion in order to look after their immediate need. The higher demand for cash with a fixed supply would certainly produce a greater return to the person motivated to save more.

One should indeed appreciate this banking mechanism that clearly works with the demand and supply theory, leaving some room for humanitarian consideration. Unlike modern banks in Canada that continue to charge unreasonably high interest on their credit cards in the midst of a deep recession with no regard for economic conditions, Chettu works with supply and demand. It is also important to note that Canadian chartered banks are not offering any easily acquired financial loans for new immigrants.

This kind of banking may be illegal to operate in the Western world; however, there are several hundred such bankers in operation in Toronto. This is how many people obtain funding to bring their relatives from Sri Lanka. With the average going rate of bringing a person from Sri Lanka at around $50,000, the responsibility of preparing passports and educating the emigrant on social, cultural, geographical and current political conditions in Canada falls to the responsibility of the illegal human smuggler. Add to that the fact that the newcomer would have to be well-informed on the nature and design of driver's licenses, health cards and the operation of the public transportation system, the illegal immigrant has to go through a more rigorous training program to adapt to life in Canada than the legal immigrant. Professional expert preparation requires time and, naturally, time costs money. Consequently, I would strongly recommend that Immigration Canada follow the same kind of preparation with new immigrants before they get exposed to the unknown.

Historically, the growth of capitalism among Protestants was found to be the greatest, not only because they believe in the idea of vindication for the suffering, but also because they acted on this idea, associated together and assisted one another with funds to ensure their individual and collective prosperity. The mentality of the Tamil people is certainly Protestant in that regard, despite the fact that most of them are born into Hindu families. Hinduism talks about the vindication of material life and not embracing material life. Among recent immigrants to Canada, I would imagine that Tamils rank at the top in terms of their achievements in capital accumulation.

In addition to the hardship of finding employment in their professional fields, Tamil immigrants also have to overcome racial discrimination in Western societies. The new immigrant lacks the necessary "connections" to find a decent job as well. So a frustrated Tamil immigrant has limited options: self-employment or operating a small business. Their new lives often begin with delivering pizza, driving taxis and, perhaps, eventually owning a taxi plate. Their second path is to be employed at three different places simultaneously, to sleep only during their breaks at work and to continue saving. Their last option is to smuggle fellow Sri Lankan Tamils into Canada, the most lucrative business of all. Everything needs capital and the Chettu is the local "bank" that offers it. The organizer of the Chettu is the local "banker", who takes the greatest risk of entrusting individuals and lending money with the hope of future regular remittance. There are many such local "bankers" that have committed suicide upon failing to recover the money from those who have withdrawn. These high risk operations are associated with even higher rewards; therefore, these entities continue to emerge in the community.

Besides the Chettu, there are a number of legal trades designed to aid in growing Tamil nationalism. In addition to this primitive financial banking system, the LTTE had to invent ways to raise capital for their projects. There are two kinds of investments; one is legal and the other is strictly illegal. Two people came to my house for the purpose of LTTE fundraising and explained to me an investment plan managed by the LTTE that guaranties returns on a fixed deposit. (I will describe this incident in the following pages.)

Commerce is a vital part of Tamil nationalism. Business owners and shopkeepers expect nationalism to create a marketplace for them to continue their support for growing Tamil nationalism. Events, such as cultural events with a decidedly LTTE flavor, are designed to bring businesses to the spotlight. The establishment of this new marketplace, unified by the idea of Tamil nationalism has evolved into a major center for the LTTE to sell their ideas to the repatriates. Retailers and marketers are the leaders in the repatriated Tamil community. These leaders earn an income that is possible only by association with the LTTE.

Just as I mentioned earlier, to display a photograph of Prabaharan in ones home gives one a level of authority, and to display the LTTE flag in ones storefront or lobby would certainly identify ones business as loyal to Tamils. In addition, one could also play the LTTE anthem or songs in the background or publicly display a tiger sculpture. All of these are a few common techniques to identify and associate one with the mainstream view. Those that do not display an overt form of Tamil nationalism are viewed with suspicion. In a worst case scenario, one can be labeled as a "traitor" and forced out of business. The entrance to my brother's house displays a tiger's face within a red circle with a red line across it. This implies a ban on Tiger activities. He openly embraced the title, "The Traitor". Despite this ban, the Tigers still attempted to fundraise there. I suppose it was one of those desperate times.

Tamil retailers and service providers pay a lump sum to the LTTE for the backing of LTTE Tamil nationalists. In return, the LTTE promotes these businesses by proclaiming them to be "agents or centers for ticket sales" and exclusive centers for the distribution of LTTE souvenirs. Although, the LTTE has not reached any solution for the Tamil issue, they have successfully created a market that serves their financial needs. In fact, they are not interested in achieving any solution to the problem, simply because the existence of the problem is important to the sound operation of this profitable market; thus, the LTTE has successfully created a remunerative market. Tamil nationalism is a convenient concept for many people to carry on their most lucrative business.

The most ridiculous aspect of the Tamil market is the media. Pure imagination and the fabrication of stories cover the media, which is supported by several full page business advertisements. The news normally only covers the LTTE and the rest of the Tamil politics are commissioned to omission. There is never a time when one hears of other political views in this so-called media. The Tamil media never even interviewed the newly-elected Chief Minister of the Eastern region or any of the other various political party leaders among Tamils. Unfortunately, following the "silence of guns", the media had no news to share about the LTTE.

The creation of a market and revenue for the LTTE agenda is confirmed by the following news report: "Diaspora funding is a major source of financing for the LTTE (Liberation Tigers of Tamil Eelam)," he wrote on March 9. "I am not sure of the exact figures at present but at one time it was reported that the LTTE raised approximately $200,000 a month from the Tamil community in Canada." (August 13th 2005, National Post)

There are two developments that could possibly offset the market: one would be to find a true solution for the long-lasting Sri Lankan problem, and the second would to somehow change consumer tastes. This change in consumer taste would be subject to many factors in the adopted countries. The question is, will the next generation of Tamils in the Western world find Tamil nationalism to be an appealing product? The answer to this question is based on the condition of our younger generation in the Western world: Have they adopted Western values? What would be the acceptance level of the mainstream society? What kind of progress do they experience in Western society? How are they influenced by their parents on Tamil politics?

The recent development of Canadian-born Tamil youth showing Tiger flags and blocking highways is certainly an alarming one that clearly highlights my speculations. This is a dangerous development for the rest of the world because of the fact that this kind of crowd could stage a relentless wave of demonstrations without being able to exert any control over its participants. This reminds me of the involvement of the Manavar Peravai--the Tamil student organization that began in the early 70's and evolved as the militant group called the LTTE. There are some Canadian Tamil youth, having been wounded in the Vanni operation, who are currently being treated in Kurunagal Hospital in Sri Lanka. In addition, there were many youth who traveled to Vanni in the past and have since returned to Canada. The nature of their visits is highly questionable. "The classified briefing says the Liberation Tigers of Tamil Eelam, better known as the LTTE or the Tamil Tigers, has approached Tamil youths in Canada to travel to Sri Lanka for weapons training." (March 21 2007, National Post)

It is important to understand that the Tamil repatriates' leaders would not have achieved their social statuses without embracing the idea of

Tamil nationalism. Likewise, repatriated businessmen would not have enjoyed their current level of access in their local markets without accommodating the idea of Tamil nationalism. Tamil criminals would not have captured the global network without aiding the LTTE. Community radio stations and newspapers that did not support Tamil nationalism would have gone bankrupt. The existence of the Western Tamil nationalists' market is essential for funding many individuals. There are a number of Tamil professionals who, finding it impossible to work with local Tamils in Toronto without associating themselves with the LTTE, have openly embraced the LTTE for financial gain. Out of this group, there are Tamil lawyers who are actively engaged in real estate practices and who also play a leading role in the local Tamil nationalist organizations in Canada. One can see these figures in the front seat of the newly-emerged LTTE organization. There are a number of figures in the present LTTE camp in Canada with a number of criminal charges, which include weapon charges. There are some Tamil lawyers highly active in the practice of safeguarding everything and anything that is associated with Tamil nationalism, including criminals.

Riot police stand in front of Tamil demonstrators after the protesters successfully blocked the Gardiner Expressway in Toronto on Sunday, May 10, 2009. (Darren Calabrese / THE CANADIAN PRESS)

The militant political agenda of Tamils, which is not endorsed by the Western states, seeks a cover to disguise their activities. The Tamil Rehabilitation Organization (TRO) has been clearly identified as one of the organizations hiding behind the banner of charity for the purpose of aiding the LTTE. One should also understand that the officials of the TRO have been active in fundraising and urging young people to join the fight for their motherland while their children continue their studies in Canada and USA. There is a prominent leading Tamil activist in the organization that has a daughter working as a medical doctor in the United States who never would have thought of sending his daughter to serve injured LTTE fighters. RCMP Counterterrorism Investigators and the Canadian Revenue Agency's charity regulators accuse the group of having ties to a group of Sri Lankan separatist guerrillas, the Liberation Tigers of Tamil Eelam, better known as the Tamil Tigers.

"We believe that there are reasonable grounds for concern that TRO (Canada) operates for purposes that conflict with Canadian public policy," the head of Canada's charities directorate wrote in a letter to the group. "More specifically, there appears to be reason to conclude that TRO (Canada) may be functioning as part of a support network for the terrorist organization Liberation Tigers of Tamil Eelam." (National Post, Thursday, Nov 20, 2008)

The idea of multiculturalism and its associated support mechanisms became a great aid to the Tamil repatriates. The influx of large numbers of Tamil refugees has strengthened the hidden agenda of the Tamil repatriates in two ways: first, it has basically outnumbered most other ethnic groups in Toronto to gain priority in receiving access to federal and provincial, as well as regional government support; secondly, it has created a solid base of powerful voters unified by the idea of Tamil nationalism and has became the most powerful bargaining tool to negotiate with various levels of governments. The mass number of politically active Tamils would cast their ballots on the orders of their local LTTE leaders. This concern was shared by this news article, according to a Party's email that was circulated:

"[Peter MacKay]'s comments have caused trouble for the seven candidates with sizeable Tamil support in and around Scarborough." "(MacKay) said exactly what Stock said about 18 months (ago)," [Sandra Buckler] wrote, "only Peter didn't know that Stock had promised not to talk about the issue during the election - yikes." "I think we have to be definitive in saying that we certainly support the Tamil community," said MacKay. "But there is a very clear and distinct line that has to be drawn when it comes to terrorist fundraising that we feel is happening in Canada right now, based on CSIS (Canadian Security Intelligence Service) reports." (January 19TH 2006, Canadian Press)

It is interesting to discover how local Tamil leaders exercise their control over these mass Tamil populations. Certainly, these leaders are able to deliver something that is not provided by any other group. In order to understand the complexity surrounding the relationship, one has to consider the condition of Tamils landing in Canada. How do local Tamil leaders gain control over and subordinate the newcomers? The newcomers are often terrified by the exposure to a new culture, new language and, moreover, their uncertainty in establishing their new life.

In the midst of this fearful experience, new Tamil immigrants fall victim to those who claim to be aiding them. While overcoming their barriers, new immigrants find that the communication barrier can be overcome only by accepting the assistance of someone who is native to their language and culture. The newcomers are not made aware of the assistance offered by the Canadian Government; rather, they are only made to believe that the help is offered by the LTTE. These workers do not proactively explain that the Canadian government is paying them. Moreover, they represent themselves as volunteers to assist Tamils on a global scale. Because of this, the newcomers often feel gratitude to these workers and give them gifts like gold jewelry, garments and food. Even then, they still feel obliged to these community workers for their entire life. This feeling of obligation leads the newcomers to obey their orders in every aspect of social relationships.

The Canadian Government grants a measure of power to these workers; however, the Canadian Government does not have the power or influence over these newcomers. In turn, these immigrants make themselves devotees of their local Tamil workers and, in due course, the workers evolve as leaders. The entire evolution of these powerhouses was systematically engineered by the LTTE from the Vanni jungle.

Sadly, the Canadian government, as well as many other Western democracies, often fall victim to political manipulation by Tamil agencies that were originally created with the sincere belief of respecting, embracing and promoting multicultural ideas.

One would find it ironic that Tamil business establishments in Toronto are functioning in full force on July 1st, Canada Day, while all Tamil business establishments are officially shut down during every official function announced by the LTTE. It is a great danger that awaits Canada by the Canadian Tamils who are not assimilated with the rest of the country and are confused by the display of leadership by local Tamils. While the government fails to take measures against this condition, the confusion keeps compounding. A ban on these organizations would not stop organizations from growing; nevertheless, a ban should be placed on the nature of their activities. The ban on the World Tamil Movement has not stopped their newspaper from being circulated. The newspaper was called "World Tamils", but a new one has emerged with the name

"Canada World Tamils". The regrettable issue here is not the inability of the Canadian government to take firm action, but it is the ability of those LTTE members who have shown the local Tamils that they are tactful, clever and resourceful in challenging Canadian laws. Canada has currently banned the following organizations:

-
- Abu Nidal Organization (ANO)
- Abu Sayyaf Group (ASG)
- Al Jihad (AJ)
- Al Qaida
- Al-Aqsa Martyrs' Brigade (AAMB)
- Al-Gama'a al-Islamiyya (AGAI)
- Al-Ittihad Al-Islam (AIAI)
- Ansar al-Islam (AI)
- Armed Islamic Group (GIA)
- Asbat Al-Ansar ("The League of Partisans")
- Aum Shinrikyo
- Autodefensas Unidas de Colombia (AUC)
- Babbar Khalsa (BK)
- Ejército de Liberación Nacional (ELN)
- Euskadi Ta Askatasuna (ETA)
- Fuerzas Armadas Revolucionarias de Colombia (FARC)
- Gulbuddin Hekmatyar
- Hamas (Harakat Al-Muqawama Al-Islamiya) («Islamic Resistance Movement»)
- Harakat ul-Mudjahidin (HuM)
- Hezb-e Islami Gulbuddin (HIG)
- Hizballah
- International Sikh Youth Federation (ISYF)
- Islamic Army of Aden (IAA)
- Islamic Movement of Uzbekistan (IMU)
- Jaish-e-Mohammed (JeM)
- Jemaah Islamiyyah (JI)
- Kahane Chai (KACH)
- Kurdistan Workers Party (PKK)
- Lashkar-e-Jhangvi (LJ)
- Lashkar-e-Tayyiba (LeT)

- **Liberation Tigers of Tamil Eelam (LTTE)**
- Mujahedin e Khalq (MEK)
- Palestine Liberation Front (PLF)
- Palestinian Islamic Jihad (PIJ)
- Popular Front for the Liberation of Palestine - General Command (PFLP-GC)
- Popular Front for the Liberation of Palestine (PFLP)
- Salafist Group for Call and Combat (GSPC)
- Sendero Luminoso (SL)
- Vanguards of Conquest (VOC)
- World Tamil Movement (WTM)

(Source:Public Safety Canada web site on 2009-06-01, http://www.publicsafety.gc.ca/prg/ns/le/cle-eng.aspx)

The dilemma is how to ban an organization that keeps evolving into a new form. The government may have banned particular organizations, but not the function of those organizations. For example, the LTTE group has evolved as a group under a different name. Secondly, the newly formed organizations are carrying out the functions that were previously carried out by the World Tamil Movement: the Tiger flag is in use, fundraising is still being conducted, and meetings and all other celebrations for the LTTE are still transpiring. Canada does not need to ban any organization; it has to ban the activities, flags, and symbols that lead to the existence of these organizations. The question and the concern of the intelligent community of Canada must be this: would it be possible for Tamil militants, that is, the LTTE elements, to turn their hostilities on the nation of Canada? The answer to this question can only be analyzed by the historical events involving the LTTE and the governments outside of the political boundaries of Sri Lanka.

The answer to this question became evident in the assassination of Rajeev Gandhi, the former Prime Minister of India. One should briefly note that India was the only country that openly came forward to support Tamil militancy and aid the Tamils in every respect; and it was India that promoted the Sri Lankan Tamil issue in the international spotlight. Historically, India was a place for our rulers and political leaders to hide even before our colonial history. There were a number of our political leaders, both Tamil and Singhalese that were hiding in South India during the fight for independence from colonization. India is the origin for the existence of Sri Lanka and, inevitably, it is the power that dictates the politics of the Island. Furthermore, in contemporary times, India is not merely a regional power, but it has evolved into an international power.

The attack on India's leader has created a lifelong obstacle in reaching a solution to Sri Lanka's problem. Sinhala nationalists attacked Rajeev Gandhi with a rifle; however, Tamil nationalists ended his life with a bomb. This remains in history as proof of the immature political wisdom of the LTTE. This particular action alarmed the international community and became the means in which Sri Lankan Tamils lost the sympathy and support of India. The majority of Sri Lankan Tamils condemns Gandhi's murder and feels the responsible parties should be brought to justice; however, the most brutal form of attack by the Sinhala nationalists, added to the unsympathetic gestures of international regimes including India, left the Tamils in Sri Lanka to take shelter under the banner of the LTTE.

One can neither deny the fact that there are a number of criminal elements within the various hierarchies of Tamil nationalism, nor reject the argument that Tamil nationalism has inherited, adopted, embraced and sheltered criminals for their mutual benefit. As the operation of the Tamil Nationalist Movement became illegal, it would not have survived in the underworld without mastering illegal skills and activities. Tamils who continue to support the LTTE are certainly misguided. The ban on the LTTE in India was brought on by the actions of the LTTE; likewise, inaction on the part of India is also the result of the LTTE's actions.

Similarly, the ban on the LTTE in Canada was also the result of activities that clearly demonstrated disrespect to the laws of this land. The ban on the LTTE and their umbrella organizations is essential to safeguard a truly multicultural society in Canada. However, constant monitoring of the various elements of the LTTE is essential as they easily manifest into something else once a ban takes effect on one particular formation. A violent culture is not an endemic feature of Tamils; it is, rather, a group among Tamils that has evolved violently. This violent group is known as the LTTE. Hence, the culture of the LTTE is not the culture of Tamils and the LTTE culture should not take precedence in the Canadian multicultural framework.

In every context, the Sri Lankan government oppresses the Tamils. It is also true that the Sri Lankan government failed to safeguard innocent Tamils during the instances when they were looted, raped, and burned alive; moreover, they were deprived of the power to determine their political destiny. Tamils were not only made refugees during the present government, they were made refugees since the time of independence from the colonial British Empire. In the past, Tamils were internal refugees. In recent times, Tamils are made to seek refuge even in North America. Most importantly, Tamils are not only the victims of Sri Lankan government brutality within the Sri Lankan political boundaries, but also the victims of the LTTE's constant torture within and beyond Sri Lankan. Tamils are not seeking the absence of war, but Tamils are seeking the presence of justice.

Prior to the Vanni war, the government and the LTTE achieved a time of peace. In the absence of war, the LTTE was afforded ample time to accumulate and build their war hardware with the help of resources from repatriates and other illegal operations. The LTTE were able to establish a condition that succeeded in uprooting the existing order for one of complete chaos. This state of anomie became an ideal ground for their survival and created conditions that would not have been possible even in a dream. It created a social disorder that succeeded in abolishing the existing order.

One can easily be misled by the display of low caste members, such as the late Mr. V. Pirabakaran and the late Mr. Tamilselvan, capturing the Tamil political leadership. This does not mean that the caste system has been abolished or is a development that should be welcomed by the progressive forces. It was similar to the situation in Iraq, where a member of the minority Sunni caste, the late Mr. Saddam Hussein, stayed in power for decades totally controlling a Shia-dominated country. During his term, he had to constantly stage wars with his neighbors to sustain the internal unity of his nation. In the absence of Saddam, the Sunni has become the oppressed group.

This demonstrates that the abolishment of the caste system is not going to take place by the act of a single person. Rather, it can only be changed through fundamental changes to the existing economic order. In order for the caste system to be eradicated, some fundamental changes must take place in the form of providing incentives for those who desire education for the purpose of renouncing their caste-based employment options. Repressive law should become much more powerful in identifying and punishing those who engage in caste-based practices. Furthermore, it is a mockery to think that Tamil nationalists, even in Canada, would not endorse their children marrying low caste Tamils while accepting a leadership that has sprouted out of the low caste. This is where one should realize that the Tamil nationalists are using the current state of militancy to defend themselves from external oppression; however, they certainly have an alternate choice of leadership for their self-government that will continue to preserve their original and inherited caste system.

Tamil nationalism would not liberate the entire Tamil population, but only one group of Tamils. This is truly a revolution by the middle class upper caste members. The lower class is only playing the role of soldiers. Ultimately, the middle class upper caste Tamils would emerge in leadership and the so-called Tamil Eelam would once again plunge into chaos.

The war on the LTTE is the right of the sovereign Sri Lankan government; however, the Sri Lankan government is destined to lose its power when it fails to equally govern an entire group of citizens. The war on the LTTE is an important one for the government; however, the political solution for the Tamils in Northern, Eastern and Central Sri Lanka; Tamil-speaking Muslims; and the Tamils as well as the Sinhalese who are marginalized based on caste, sexual orientation, and any other basis of exclusion, must be delivered protection in the form of a new constitution. This is the only way to create a harmonious society in Sri Lanka. To prevent future chaos, the solution should not only address the Tamil issue, but it has to clearly stipulate a solution for the entire nation. Undoubtedly, one can say that such a solution would also bankrupt the LTTE elements in Canada and the rest of the Western world. Notwithstanding, because the nation continues to shed the blood of so many of its people, the political solution must then serve the entire nation.

Under the clouds of Tamil nationalism, there are a number of criminal elements and their lawyers that continue to operate in Western countries. "Toronto Police are still probing any possible link between an alleged debit-card scam they broke up over the weekend and an-FBI- led international terror investigation that involved 13 suspects in Canada and the

U.S. last week believed to be procuring arms for the Liberation Tigers of Tamil Eelam..." (National Post, August 29, 2006).

Human smuggling agents operating in Canada, earning $50,000 CAD per person; fundraising both through legitimate and illegitimate means, with the proceeds going to the underworld economy; unimaginable social statuses enjoyed by those who openly identify themselves as representatives of the LTTE; expropriation from temples, restaurants, and textile stores; all of this has been justified in the name of seeking freedom. Let us look at a few specific examples.

An unconfirmed report states that, following the downfall of the LTTE, there was a large scale human smuggling operation carried out by the LTTE with the help of shipping liners. In regard to expropriation, confiscated establishments would either be registered under the name of LTTE members or sympathizers, or would simply become the personal property of the current registered owner. In the absence of strong LTTE leadership in Sri Lanka, the current owners of the expropriated property would have to compete with other LTTE supporters and sympathizers.

Thus, one can see a new class of wealthy Tamils emerging in the Tamil diaspora as a result of the LTTE defeat in Sri Lanka. On the issue of fundraising, I had a personal experience with two members of the LTTE: one identified himself as "Mathakal Kannan", and the second one identified himself as "Thiru". Thiru was also a former member of the PLOTE and he was stationed in the "Thenee camp" in the Mathurai district of Tamil Nadu, India. Their legal names and addresses were recorded by the Durham Regional Police. The story was published in "The Toronto Star" as follows: "Street level" fundraising for the terrorist organization continues, Becker said. Following visits by two members who identified themselves as raising funds for the terrorist organization, Rajan Mahavalirajan called the police. The men told Mahavalirajan, a business owner, that they were collecting money on behalf of the organization to buy surface-to-air missiles in Sri Lanka."(Toronto Star, Dec 06, 2006 09:13 AM)

Following the incident involving the LTTE member's fundraising activity at my home, the incident was documented by the Human Rights Watch. This caused the LTTE media to stage their usual fabricated propaganda on me to divert the real story of their fundraising attempts. In their article, I was portrayed as a parent of two adopted children named Gandhi and Stalin. In fact, that part of the story is true that I am the parent of these "children"; however, they had also added that I was abusive to them, which was not true. In truth, these "children" are highly abusive to me; however, the Children's Aid Society cannot be involved in this case. Gandhi was my oldest "son", my pet white rabbit. He passed away at the age of eight. I buried him in my backyard and decorated his tomb with a memorial stone and a statue of Buddha surrounded by a flower garden. My second son, Stalin, a German Shepherd dog, continues to live his royal life at the age of seven. In fact, Mr. Stalin gave "Mathakal Kannan" and "Thiru" a wonderful reception when they stopped by our home to fundraise. In the future, should anyone ever be concerned about the wellbeing of my "son", they should feel free to contact the Durham Region Animal Services or the Blue Cross, but most certainly not the Children's Aid Society.

At this point, I am obligated to reproduce said article published on a pro-LTTE website as follows:

Tuesday, 12 December 2006

In 1982 after murdering Tamil youths, escaped to Canada, where he was washed of his murders and granted visa. – Who is Mahavalirajan. Mahavalirajan is the son of former Sri Lankan Communist Party member and founder of the Senthamilar Militant organization, V. Ponnambalam. Mahavalirajan was influenced by his father's militant politics to join the PLOT paramilitary group in Sri Lanka. During the early 80's he served as field commander for that group.

In 1982 after murdering two Tamil youths, Iraikumaran and Umaikumaran, of the Tamil Students Association, Mahavalirajan escaped to Canada, where he was washed of his murders and granted visa.

The murderer seems to have found a safe heaven in a leafy Ontario suburb, where astonishingly he has managed to adopt two Canadian children. The police and social services seem to be rather too happy with two children in the hands of a paramilitary member and murderer.

Having maintained a low profile to avoid being spotted by relatives of the two students he had murdered, Mahavalirajan has reappeared on the Tamil community's arena with bogus claims that the Liberation Tigers of Tamil Eelam (LTTE) had asked him for funds to buy anti-air craft missiles.

Even worse, Ms. Jo Becker of Human Rights Watch (HRW) and some pseudo journalists in Toronto seem to think that the LTTE would actually ask a PLOT member for funding. Many Tamils say that Ms. Jo Becker is receiving back hand payments from the Government of Sri Lanka (GoSL). They cite her poorly researched, un-scientific, 'dodgy' claims about LTTE 'Funding the Final War' by 'extorting' money from Tamil Diaspora; her zero attention to the abduction of 13 and 14 year old children by Sri Lankan armed forces for the Karuna paramilitary group; and her close connections to paramilitary criminals such as V. Rama-raj who is currently in a high security prison in Switzerland.

Despite thousands of complaints, the HRW, a renowned human rights organization has failed to investigate Ms Becker and has continued to let her tarnish the organization's name. Neither has the Canadian government taken any action to save the two children whom the murderer Mahavalirajan had adopted."

This episode and the false propaganda surrounding it remind me of the idea advocated by the Italian Fascist leader, the late Mr. Mussolini. He said that the people don't have to know it, but they should believe it. We create the faith in them to believe that mountains can be moved. The illusion of a "Movable Mountain" becomes a reality over time. This form of propaganda was very common among the LTTE and their affiliated organizations. Unfortunately, the illusion not only obscured the LTTE supporters, it also blinded the LTTE leadership from seeing the reality.

In addition, the Tamil community's local radio stations are in the hands of the LTTE. The whole operation is meticulously programmed by the LTTE. Any Tamil community local radio station that fails to broadcast LTTE programming is subjected to coercive force. Recently, the hardware of a Toronto Tamil radio station was expropriated overnight for the owner's failure to remain loyal to the LTTE. Although the radio station served the LTTE, it failed to fully comply with the LTTE propaganda standard. The announcer from the radio station said, "Imagine the people living in Vanni, if this had happened here."

Sunday Tamil schools are other interesting places that have been systematically programmed to corrupt young Tamil learners. On one occasion, a teacher was imparting to the young students that the action of a young Tamil girl who was to marry a non-Tamil should be regarded as a great betrayal to her mother and the motherland. The teacher then began sharing an upper class and upper caste Jaffna Tamil mentality. Jaffna Tamils do not respect Tamils married to the Sinhalese, Indian Tamils, and low castes. It would be interesting to see how many Canadian-born or Canadian-raised children of Tamils have betrayed their mother and motherland. The Chief of Police for the LTTE himself, the late Mr. Nadesan, was married to a Sinhala lady who died with him in Vanni. Moreover, it was a self-destructive policy on the basis that the so-called "Voice of the Nation", the late Mr. Anton Balasingam, had himself betrayed his mother and the Tamil motherland by marrying an Australian White woman.

This kind of political ideology is equally as dangerous as Nazi ideology. The fact that such thinking prevails among the teachers of Sunday Tamil schools is certain to spread the seeds of hatred. It was on this issue that I raised my concern to various police divisions in a community meeting organized by various Toronto police divisions. There was a Tamil lawyer there arguing that non-acceptance of cross-cultural marriages is not considered a hate crime. Although, I agree with him according to existing laws, even this lawyer knew that such a condition is a clear display of a covert form of hatred towards other races. The Sunday Tamil school teacher and the lawyer who came to her defense were clearly acting as "moral entrepreneurs". Their "moral panic" on the issue of changing social trends is also a clear concern of upper caste Tamils. Their desire for a "pure Tamil race" would meet the same destiny as Adolf Hitler's.

The following reveals the concern of some Canadians: "If domestic politics lurk behind Canada's too-supple position, then Liberals might well be insulting the very community to which they're trying to pander.

No doubt most Tamils in Canada support their countrymen at home, not quite a fifth of Sri Lanka's 20 million people. Before and since the start of guerrilla warfare and terrorism, Tamils have suffered greatly. But we don't believe the majority of Tamils in this country are truly enthusiastic about the LTTE's methods. If they are, we have a serious problem." (The Gazette, Montreal, Que.: Mar 15, 2005, P. A22).

Whether it was the previous leadership or the current one, both have no interest in sending their children to the Tamil homeland to join the fight. Upon further exploration, one would find that these leaders and their children enjoy well-to-do lifestyles in the Western world; however, they are always interested in other people's children. They justify their actions by claiming that they have volunteered their time and money for the freedom fight, instead of giving it to their children. Those who do not give should give their sons for freedom. This was the same idea that existed long ago where, in the absence of a horse, one would give ones son to the fight. This fight was organized by Tamil middle class intellectuals and the capitalists among us. They would never die for it; they only invest in it. They invest to earn a good return; however, they are able to accept any loss because they can survive and reinvest in the political struggle. Those who die are only low class and low caste! The actual soldiers without horses to donate had to come to the battlefield. According to the press, "The classified briefing says the Liberation Tigers of Tamil Eelam, better known as the LTTE or the Tamil Tigers, has approached Tamil youths in Canada to travel to Sri Lanka for weapons training." (March 21st 2007, National Post)

The recent development of Tamil youth in Canada and North America becoming involved in the protest marches clearly shows that the real culprits of this well-organized agitation want to stay only in the background. This particular development reminds me of the student organization, Manavar Peravai, of the early 1970's. The formation of this student group was the creation of Tamil militants. It was organized to carry out the political agenda of the Tamil nationalist politicians and to find more fertile ground as the government's educational policies affected post-secondary studies. The educational policy on post-secondary studies was introduced and called "standardization".

The real purpose of this policy is to aid students from backward areas to enter universities. The students are educated with limited resources in the underdeveloped areas of the country. This was not aimed at eliminating Tamil youth from entering universities, but this was a measure that affected Tamils as well as Sinhalese from the developed areas of the country. The middle class Tamils, who could only dream of their children becoming doctors and engineers, registered their children as residents of some of those underdeveloped areas of the country. The nationalist Tamil politicians were able to take advantage of this situation. The frustration that prevailed among the urban Tamil students turned them into a newly-emerged political force. The student organization grew quickly in numbers as thrills and excitement always welcome young blood. While this formation started staging a number of illegal and criminal activities, Tamil nationalist politicians stayed in the background and watched. Finally, we, the Tamils, created a generation of young Tamils who never attended universities or ever had any form of schooling. Young Tamil children as early as eight had been forced to take up arms and die.

I regret to see that same event is unfolding among us in Canada. The night the protestors in Toronto blocked the highway, one of the directors of the Tamil Congress, Mr. David Poobalapillai was resting at home and watching TV as he would have nothing to do with this illegal activity. He gave an interview on CP24, a local Toronto TV station, from his residence. The Tamil Congress in Canada should have openly condemned the highway protest. They should also have condemned the activity of displaying the Tiger flag in the midst of the White House protest. It was an irresponsible act on Mr. Poobalapillai's part to stay home and watch TV.

This again reminds me of the situation in Sri Lanka where Tamil youth groups would engage in some sort of illegal form of protest and get into trouble while the Tamil nationalist politicians would not condemn or prevent it from happening. The Tamil Congress never issued a press release urging the Tamils in Canada to refrain from the fundraising activities for LTTE; nevertheless, Mr. Poobalapillai did appeal to the Tamil community to identify the culprit behind the murder of a young boy in Scarborough, my relative. While I appreciate his efforts to find his murderers, I wonder why he failed to act with the same responsibility for other criminal events such as the attack on a Buddhist temple, the burning of a Sinhala restaurant in Brampton and the brutal attack on a number of Tamil journalists in Scarborough for speaking against LTTE.

Here is a letter from the Progressive Tamil Congress that was sent to Tamil associations in Canada, including the Tamil Congress:

Progressive Tamil Congress- Canada

canadaptc@gmail.com

February 23, 2009

To: All Organizers of White House demonstration

Dear Sir,

We, the Progressive Tamil Congress of Canada urge you and other Tamil Organizations to renounce the position of supporting LTTE and join to take appropriate measures to win the aspirations of Tamils in Sri Lanka. Clearly, the undiplomatic political action of LTTE and irrational as well as mere emotional demonstrations of Tamil repatriates led to an unfavorable, unsympathetic political stand by the Western governments.

Despite the diminishing international support for LTTE and their cruelty for its' own people, you and a few other organizations continue to believe and demonstrate things that are further harmful to Tamils in Sri Lanka. A typical example was the recent demonstration in front of the White House, where there were people with the LTTE flag carrying pictures of Pirabakaran, was organized as a demonstration for the humanitarian needs of Tamils in "Wani". The incident reveals that it was organized under the banner of humanitarian catastrophe to mask the real identity of LTTE.

You have not only concealed your program from the people who joined you, you have also taken their voice for granted with regards to LTTE. The call for demonstration never mentioned anything about LTTE or their association to this demonstration; however, you permitted the demonstrators to carry LTTE flag and pictures of Pirabakaran on the buses. We have learnt that the Transportation companies, which came to know about your involvement, had cancelled their commitment to you at the last minute. Consequently, there were about one thousand people who became stranded in front of the pick up points. Furthermore, you had put the lives of those joined to you in jeopardy by demonstrating with banners of LTTE in a country where LTTE is considered a terrorist group. It is our understanding that you and your association with LTTE have not only put our Sri Lankan Tamils in a dreadful situation, this condition is now extended to Tamils in Greater Toronto Area. Therefore, you should be held liable for your irresponsible actions. We hope that you will soon remedy the situation by adopting true practices to safeguard the interest of Tamils in Sri Lanka and not the LTTE.

Thank you,

Yours truly,

Rajan Mahavalirajan

(Coordinator)

Although, we never received any reply to this letter, we noticed that the organizers intensified their display of LTTE flags and pictures of Pirabaharan. It produced a very strong disapproval among Canadians. Tamil nationalist leaders emerged as defense lawyers for the accused. The accused were called "heroes" while the nationalist politicians received the credit for saving the "hero". Ultimately, the nationalist politicians emerged head and shoulders above the "heroes".

In the recent protests, one cannot see any familiar faces in these illegal activities. They were not spontaneous; they were pre-planned well-executed acts of a criminal gang. Prior to this incident, the incident of blocking the highway was, in their minds, discussed on a Tamil community radio show. They came up with some new names as organizers for these events. They were very careful not to use the names of existing organizations. I believe that radio stations should keep copies of their broadcasts for a certain period and then by reviewing the tape they would be able to find the truth regarding these events. There are Tamil organizations that brought this to the attention of the interested parties in Canada. The youth gangs are driven by mere emotion; but, on the contrary, the real culprits act with a clear goal in mind. Their goal is to become the future political candidates of major parties in Canada. Some would run with the Liberals, others with the NDP, and a few with the Conservatives; however, they are all from the same camp working for the LTTE. There is nothing wrong with promoting oneself, but one should not victimize a race or group of people in the name of "self-actualization".

The gradual annihilation of the LTTE's top leadership is the direct result of their failure to handle their conflict with diplomacy. This has caused a major division among LTTE members at home as well as abroad. The international spokesperson for the LTTE, (K. P.) Patmanapan, has officially declared the death of their supreme leader, V. Prabaharan; however, this has been denied by LTTE leadership in Tamil Nadu, India. Mr. Nadumaran, a former member of the Indian Parliament, jointly with V. Kopalasamy, have come forward and called K. P. a traitor. This internal conflict over the death of Prabaharan could further split the LTTE into smaller groups. There are people who do not believe that Mr. Prabaharan has died and they continue to believe in the resurrection of the LTTE. On the contrary, there are people who believe that the LTTE leadership has been totally annihilated and the fight for self-rule is over.

In the midst of these opposing speculations, there are a few other reasons why the fight for independence should take a new direction. The new direction would neither be an arms struggle nor hopeless negotiations with the Sri Lankan government. The new direction is called "the third option". In fact, the third option is not completely new; it was the only hope we had between the early 80's and the late 90's. The country that is capable of bringing change to the existing situation is India. The annihilation of the LTTE is the result of the arrogance and ignorance that prevailed among the LTTE and their global supporters.

The day that the LTTE attacked Indian interests, particularly with the murder of former Prime Minister, Rajeev Gandhi, the LTTE terminated the long-standing traditional goodwill that existed between Sri Lankan Tamils and India. There are some people who are wondering why India does not show any forgiveness. The answer for them is that there are different types of crimes leading to different types of punishment. Some lead to short-term imprisonment, some lead to life imprisonment and others lead to capital punishment. The kind of crime the late Mr. Praba-haran committed was the kind that leads to capital punishment. What we witnessed in Vanni was the execution of that punishment.

At this juncture, the status of Prabaharan is irrelevant to our struggle, and the protest rallies in the Western world are also a wasteful use of our resources: earning the goodwill of India is the only option we have. Fol-lowing the defeat of the LTTE, one can see that Sinhala nationalism is growing at a rapid rate. This growth could certainly serve to undermine the possibility of any political settlement and it could produce an exter-nally forced solution that is highly undesired by Sinhala nationalists. As the international community investigates the subject of war crimes, the President of Sri Lanka has declared that he carried out the war for India. This statement unequivocally shows the involvement of India in this war.

There are Tamils, like me, who would agree to a war launched against the LTTE; however, even we find it is difficult to accept the humiliation and the cost of this war, particularly, the loss of innocent lives. Even the anti-LTTE Tamil would find it is hard to digest the scene of Prabaharan's mud-caked body lying naked. Humiliating a dead person would not do any good for the future of our country. Similarly, the scene of the naked bodies of LTTE fighters, paraded around the Sinhalese villages after their successful suicide attack on the Anurajapura Sri Lankan airbase, was a barbaric act committed by the Sri Lankan government.

Perhaps, the government of Sri Lanka should learn from the historical account of Elara and Dutugemunu. The victorious Dutugemunu built a temple for the defeated Tamil king Elara and ordered every passerby to pay respect to him. Prabaharan does not deserve a temple, but he does not deserve humiliation either. The death of Prabaharan was not caused by any external party; it was the work of his supporters who never ever con-demned the killing of any of his political opponents. Instead, they praised him for the subtle nature of the act and credited him for his clever way of execution. This made him believe his supporters were wholeheartedly with him and his supporters were quite capable of convincing the interna-tional community of this. Thus, he was given a contrived leadership and ultimately was betrayed by his own people.

The display of the LTTE flags in the midst of demonstrations further repelled the international community. There are rumors in the community that say that this was a well-planned act by those who were actively involved in fundraising to prevent the LTTE from ever coming to claim the fortune that they had collected. As a result of the LTTE downfall, a new class has emerged with unclaimed gold and currency. One can also clearly anticipate some form of rivalry in appropriating these riches which could lead to a violent conflict to repossess the stockpile.

With regard to the downfall of Prabaharan, the second factor was that the over- praised leadership had lost the sense to recognize the reality of their strength. The majority of Tamils in the Western world embraced Prabaharan's political dictatorship and associated with his ruthless acts. They produced songs where Prabaharan was described as another reincarnation of the God, Krishna, and depicted him as being equal to the God, Murugan. The song portrays Prabaharan as an indestructible supernatural being. This idea had convinced Prabaharan that he was a supernatural being and beyond destruction; thus, he exposed himself to "inescapable danger".

Lastly, the wealthy repatriates, Tamil professionals with intellectual capacities, some politicians from Tamil Nadu, and international Tamil criminals all as one voice told him that they would not fail to protect him. Prabaharan and his carders had blind faith in this group of misguided political opportunists. The last phone conversation that took place between Prabaharan and K. P., the person responsible for the international affairs of the LTTE, can reveal the facts about different promises made by the foreign-based LTTE leaders regarding his safety.

The shift of leadership in the Tamil organizations of the Tamil diaspora and the emergence of new organizations to compete with the existing ones are on the horizon. New faces will soon replace the old ones; however, the leadership role of Tamil Canadian youth is certainly taking the same path as the Manavar Peravai did. There are a number of Tamil youth who have had to skip their classes to attend to the political agenda set by the LTTE and the repatriates seeking political leadership in their adopted countries. The demonstrations are a display of the vehemently driven Tamil youths.

One can certainly expect some sort of irrational activity to embark from this formation. Incidents like the Buddhist temple attack in Scarborough and the Sinhala restaurant attacks were only a token of what we are about to witness, unless the governments in Canada take very firm action against these groups. No one would ever challenge or deny the political aspirations of the growing Tamil professionals in Canada; however, the use of Tamil nationalism along with the misuse of Tamil youth in Canada has to be condemned. The late Mr. Prabaharan can be regarded as both a perpetrator and a victim of a mass crime. He was a perpetrator when he took the leadership role to execute the plan; at the same time, he should be considered a victim by the middle class upper caste political opportunist.

One can be cynical and ask why the Sri Lankan government is refusing the entry of foreign NGO's to the post-Vanni war zone. One could speculate a number of things; for example, one may say that the government is still in the process of concealing war crime evidence. Perhaps, there were a number of foreign troops engaged in the war and they continued to stay and explore the remains of the LTTE. There are a number of theories floating around the Tamil diaspora regarding what happened leading to the death of Prabaharan. His clean-shaven face coupled with his ironed military uniform would make one suspect that he had been there to surrender.

The Indian Peace Keeping Operation was a failed operation for India and a missed opportunity for the Tamils in Sri Lanka. It was the LTTE that caused the failure of an Indian-mediated settlement. The LTTE was keen on securing an undisputed sole-leadership over Tamil politics. The role of India, along with their actions, is not a topic for debate. It can only be handled by our moderate politicians with diplomatic experience.

Protest rallies continued all around the world as the government forces closed in.

In the absence of Prabaharan and his hard-line approach, one could expect the role of India in the negotiation process to revive and settle Sri Lanka's problems for good. It is the noble task of all Tamil political leaders to reach a workable agreement and form a unitary form of organization to gain a self-government that would work within the frame work of a federal Sri Lankan constitution. This unitary regional self-government should evolve with the North and the East together; however, in the absence of an agreement with the Eastern provincial leaders; it could evolve as two separate states. These states could have their choice of a name, such as Tamil Eelam.

The question of hill country Tamils should also be addressed and their aspirations should be settled in the form of self-government. It would become inevitable for Sri Lanka to resolve the problem in a peaceful manner to avoid the involvement of foreign powers dividing the country. Sinhala nationalists must yield to the legitimate grievances of all minorities in the country. In the midst of all of these negotiations, one should not neglect the grievances of Muslims in the country. We, the Tamil repatriates, should work to gain the trust of our adopted countries by disengaging ourselves from the criminal elements within us. At this point, it is appropriate to present the letter I recently sent to all the political leaders of Canada:

30/04/2009

Dear fellow Canadians,

As a Tamil Canadian living in proximity to the Greater Toronto Region, I have the following to share with you. The demonstration staged by a large mobilization of the Tamils in and around our vital points of economy for a prolonged period has not created sympathy to the Tamils' political aspiration; on the contrary, it has negatively impacted on many ordinary citizens of this country. Consequently, it has resulted in an unsympathetic, moreover, confrontational stand with the mainstream society. Therefore, as a Tamil Canadian, I strongly express my condemnation of these so called "attention rallies."

In every protest, we know that the key figures would only stay in the background of the scene, and appear only if and when the active members on the ground requested help. The key members of this protest have their own agenda. One group of key members are interested in mobilizing the support of this mass Tamil population for the purpose of their entry into Canadian politics. The second group of key members are interested in becoming millionaires over the issue of Tamil nationalism. Above all, there is the LTTE manipulating these parties for their political manoeuvring; the LTTE, as a banned organization requires the support of the above the parties to disguise their function. It is common sense for one to understand that this illegal organization could generate funds through illegal activities. As such being the case, the fundraisers for LTTE are engaged in a number of illegal activities, namely, human smuggling, extortion, drug trafficking, credit card duplication and money laundering. The key members, who actively aided LTTE with this illegally generated money working on a 30% commission, have become greedy to possess the entire portion of the collection. In order for them to inherit illegally collected millions of dollars, they too wish to see that the LTTE is totally annihilated.

The interest of the middle class intellectual Tamils with their desire to enter Canadian politics coupled with the second group of key members, who become millionaires through illegal activities; emerged as a new social status group in Tamil Diasporas. This situation is very similar to the one we had in Jaffna, Sri Lanka about thirty years ago. The Tamil nationalist political leaders, who were lawyers by profession, associated themselves with underworld members from Valvettithurai. Valvettithurai is the birth place of Mr. Pirabakaran and he worked under the leadership of Mr. Kuttimani who was actively engaged in smuggling and other forms of underworld activities. The bond created among the Tamil nationalist politicians and the underworld members was a marriage of convenience. The underworld went on and murdered the political rivals of the Tamil nationalist politicians, while the Tamil nationalist politicians appeared as defence lawyers for the criminals.

The question, or rather the puzzle here is, how do we differentiate or distinguish the key players from the general population that is only emotionally connected to these "attention rallies?" The middle class Tamil intellectuals who appeared front stage addressing the crowds would be keen on drawing the attention of the Tamil mass and like to see their involvements in every Tamil function indiscriminately. These are the very people, who use the idea of bilingualism, to release two different contradicting statements in two different languages. One in English, talks about human rights violation, and the other one in Tamil embrace the LTTE ideology. Unlike this, the underworld members would only look after the funding aspect of these events. Their monetary contribution is as large a sum as one could imagine the dollar value required to transport large number of Tamils from every part of Canada to Ottawa and Washington, DC. The underworld members are the backbone for these events and they are very capable of staging any form of terror in any part of this world.

The Western countries are in the midst of a dilemma on how to resolve the issue of "attention rallies" without sacrificing the democratic values and the civil rights of their citizens. As the federal and provincial governments struggle to function in the midst of the current recession, the "attention rallies" have overburdened the economy to achieve its' normalcy.

I suggest that the Canadian government issue a public statement including in Tamil. The message should be both televised and broadcasted in Tamil media. The content should reflect the following:

The Tamils in Canada should be asked to cooperate with the rest of the nation to overcome the current economic crisis by disengaging their activities that are hindering the economic activities of the society.

The limitations of the Canadian government, in terms of dealing with the affairs of a sovereign state like Sri Lanka, must be clearly explained to Tamil repatriates in Tamil as well As the displeasure of the Canadian government in seeing the LTTE flags in a crowd that was largely gathered to earn sympathy for the Tamil civilians. The approach to the Tamil issue is different from the approach to the LTTE.

The LTTE remains a banned organization in Canada and the LTTE leaders are wanted in India on murder charges. Furthermore, they are facing many other charges classified under war crimes.

The Canadian government should assure the Tamils in Canada that it would set up a peace mission to Sri Lanka to oversee the operation of Tamil settlement and their needs. Subsequently, the government should take the leadership role to mediate a political settlement partnering the neighbour India.

On the issue of criminal activities carried out in the name of Tamil nationalism, the Law enforcement units in Canada should take an active role in identifying the nature of crime, members of the criminal groups and the assets obtained through these criminal activities.

The Tamils in Canada should help law enforcement to identify the criminals in the Tamil community. There must be a hotline set up for the Tamils to report illegal activities in the community, particularly, the kind of criminal activities done in the name of Tamil nationalism. The communication has to be also in Tamil.

The organizations, business people, temple owners, trustees, Tamil lawyers and other professionals should be called for a meeting to explain the legal consequences for being involved in such illegal activities.

Their input on the issue of dealing with this crisis should be recorded. They should all be asked to display a banner published by law enforcements on the Tamil hotline for crime reporting.

As an incentive, the informants should be compensated for the information. The level of compensation should fluctuate on the value of information. This was a tactic used by the intelligence on biker gangs. The information led to the arrest of a number of members on global scale.

A website should be established for the purpose of crime reporting. This should also be connected to CCRA site. Most crimes are tax-related crimes; therefore, it is appropriate to pass on the information to Revenue Canada for their investigation.

Rajan Mahavalirajan

rajanmahavalirajan@yahoo.ca"

THE FUTURE OF THE TAMIL NATION:
NOT A FOREGONE CONCLUSION

The Tamils in Sri Lanka and the Tamils in the Tamil diaspora would be able to understand the role of India through the analogy of a Hindu folk tale. On one fine occasion, Lord Siva asked his children to go around the world and he said that the first one to complete the circumnavigation would be awarded with a delicious mango. Lord Murugan went flying around the world with his peacock while the God, Pillyar, circled around his parents, Lord Siva and the Goddess, Uma Devi. His explanation was that parents are the world for their children. Therefore, children do not have to physically go around the world. The same can be achieved by going around the parents.

In like manner, Tamils need to follow this path. They don't have to go around the world and engage in an "attention rally"; they only have to rally in India--the world is there. It was India that brought us to the international spotlight since 1981, and it was India that brought the arrogant, ignorant and terroristic Tamil leadership down. Thus, India has the power to resolve and reconcile. Our third option and our last option is India.

Tamil repatriates should completely abandon LTTE ideologies and identification and come up with a common-ground approach to embrace all Tamils including Muslims to create pressure for a permanent political settlement for all minorities in Sri Lanka. The issue of war crimes is an important one for all to deal with. We certainly have to identify the individuals from the government side as well as the LTTE side that participated in crimes against humanity. The Sri Lankan government has to draft new legislations to curtail the spread of Sinhala nationalism.

There is nothing to cerebrate in this war; we have only killed our own people for something we forced them to fight for; we are all responsible for what happened. A figure like Prabaharan did not emerge out of a vacuum; he was a product of our own manifestation. The anger of Tamils along with the frustrations on their long-neglected political grievances clustered around militant Tamil nationalism and reified as the LTTE. The failure to attend to this issue would undoubtedly divide this country even more.

For the future success of Sri Lanka in the post-LTTE era, there are few immediate issues need to be addressed: One of these issues is the plight of the Tamil civilians who have been held hostage by the LTTE since the onset of the latest military operation in Mulaithevu ended in May of 2009. Caging these innocent 260,000 Tamil civilians--mainly children and seniors, in poorly structured makeshift camps will only lead to hostility. They should be freed to resume their normal lives. As their traditional homeland is not safe enough for them to occupy, the government should create immediate settlement projects elsewhere.

The second issue involves LTTE carders who were caught during the Mulaithevu operation. They must be rehabilitated; however, they should only be freed into a Tamil federal state and a rehabilitated Sri Lankan society. Freeing them into the current political situation of Sri Lanka would only make them take arms up again. Thus, rehabilitation is not only a need for the carders, but for the country as a whole. Any one from the captured group, indicate any interest to pursue their goals outside the country, should be freed to travel. International community should not treat them as terrorist, but victims of an unjust war. There are many human rights organizations published reports on child recruitment, and forceful recruitment by LTTE. On this basis, the captured fighters, perhaps, did not contribute to the war voluntarily.

On the Canadian front, we need to acknowledge and address the current treatment of Mr. Bob Rae, a Liberal member of the parliament in Canada: it was a highly undiplomatic, arrogant and ignorant act by the Sri Lankan government. The Sri Lankan government has insulted a very legitimate contributor to solving our problem. He is involved in this issue for many years and his stand is neutral. He has condemned the actions of the LTTE and he has questioned the effects of the war on innocent Tamil civilians. Perhaps, I should repeat the question that I had asked him during a fundraising dinner for his Liberal leadership. The question was, "Would you consider having a diplomatic ban along with some trade embargo on Sri Lanka?" His answer to this question was, "no"; however, having deported by the Sri Lankan government, has he changed his mind?

I have a great respect for Mr. Bob Rae and many minorities in the province of Ontario were benefited during his government. He instituted some excellent social programs and he is one of those individuals that could make changes in Sri Lanka. He is neither anti-government nor anti-LTTE. He is unbiased and just in mind.

We, the Tamil repatriates, should urge foreign governments to pressure our native government of Sri Lanka for a political settlement at the earliest possible time frame. The pressure should come along with a trade embargo and diplomatic restrictions on Sri Lanka. International community had successfully pressured the South African government to adopt radical change to the apartheid regime. The labor unrest created by the trade embargo would certainly engage every citizen, beyond racial identification, to take part in the fight against inequality. The capitalist in the country have successfully diverted the attention of the working class on race issue; however, it is time to bring class issue to the spot light.

The few Sinhala leftist leaders from the Lanka Sama Samaja Party (LSSP), who fought for the rights of Tamils and violently attacked by the Sinhala nationalist, should be remembered and their dream should be attained. Their bravery and sacrifice for the rights of Tamils was commendable. There were some left without arm and few were crippled. Thus, our fight is not a fight of an ethnic group, but it is a fight of our nation including all citizens of Sri Lanka.

The Canadian government should undertake the responsibility to deport those who are engaged in criminal activities with criminal agenda in the name of Tamil nationalism. This group is certainly undermining the peace process in Sri Lanka.

I would like to end this work with the following passage from the writings of former Canadian Prime Minister Pierre Elliott Trudeau:

"In the world today, when whole groups of so called sovereign states are experimenting with rational forms of integration, the exercise of sovereignty will not only be divided within federal states; it will have to be further divided between the states and the communities of the states. If this tendency is accentuated the very idea of national sovereignty will recede and, with it, the need for an emotional justification such as nationalism. International law will no longer be explained away as so much "positive international morality"; it will be recognized as the true law, a "coercive order... for the promotion of peace".

Bibliography

1. Chelvadurai Manogaran (2000). The Untold Story Of Ancient Tamils In Sri Lanka: Sri Lanka: Kumaran Publishers.

2. Malik, Kennedy and Oberst (1987,1991,199 1998). Government & Politics in South Asia. United States Of America/ United Kingdom: WestView Press, A Member of Perseus Books.

3. S. Ponniah (1983). The truth vs. "This is the Truth": A Reply: Sri Lanka: Yarl Punithavajan Katholica Atchchakam.

4. Pierre Elliott Trudeau (1968). Federalism and the French Canadians: Toronto Canada: The T.H. Best Printing Company Limited.

5. Ponmalar (September 1994)

6. Tarzie Vittachi (1958). Emergency 58: The Story of The Ceylon Riots. London W1: Ebenezer Baylis and Son Limited.

7. Canadian Press January 19th 2006.

8. Canadian press May 10th 2009.

9. National Post (Toronto) August 13th 2005.

10. National Post (Toronto) August 29th 2006.

11. National Post (Toronto) March21st 2007.

12. National Post (Toronto) November 20th 2008.

13. The Gazette. Montreal, Que.: Mar 15, 2005. p.A22).

14. Toronto Star December 06th 2006.

15. The Public Safety Canada web site on 2009-06-01 http://www.publicsafety.gc.ca/prg/ns/le/cle-eng.aspx

16. "In 1982 after murdering Tamil youths, escaped to Canada, where he was washed of his murders and granted visa. – Who is Mahavalirajan." Nitharsanam August 05th 2009. http://www.nitharsanam.com/?nav=6005

17. http://mymastersvoice.org

Special Thanks

1. To my friend and the president of the Progressive Tamil Congress, Mr. U. Baskaran, a former member of the Sri Lankan Parliament and a member of the EPDP, for encouraging me to write this book.

2. To the professors of Trent University. They made me see this world differently.

3. To the publisher, Author House.

4. To Mr. Chandrakumar Nitharsan for the cover design.

5. To my copy editor, Stacy DeIrish of Print Ready Editing & Design, and to Senchsamudra Namunakulan for photo arrangement.

6. Lastly, to my family for their tolerance and co-operation during this project.